Achieving **QTLS**

Managing Behaviour
in Further and Adult Education

Third Edition

Achieving **QTLS**

Managing Behaviour
in Further and Adult Education

Third Edition

Susan Wallace

Los Angeles | London | New Delhi
Singapore | Washington DC

Acknowledgements

The author would like to acknowledge the help of all those teachers and learners in further education colleges who participated in the research projects that underpin the information in this book, and to thank Isabella Wallace for her input and feedback on some of these ideas and strategies.

SAGE | Learning Matters

Los Angeles | London | New Delhi
Singapore | Washington DC

Learning Matters
An imprint of SAGE Publications Ltd
1 Oliver's Yard
55 City Road
London
EC1Y 1SP

SAGE Publications Inc.
2455 Teller Road
Thousand Oaks, California 91320

SAGE Publications India Pvt Ltd
B 1/I 1 Mohan Cooperative Industrial Area
Malthura Road
New Delhi 110 044

SAGE Publications Asia-Pacific Pte Ltd
3 Church Street
#102-04 Samsung Hub
Singapore 049483

Editor: Amy Thornton
Development editor: Clare Weaver
Production controller: Chris Marke
Project management: Deer Park Productions, Tavistock
Marketing manager: Catherine Slinn
Cover design: Wendy Scott
Typeset by: Pantek Media, Maidstone, Kent
Printed by: Henry Ling Limited at the Dorset Press, Dorchester DT1 1HD

© 2013 Susan Wallace

First published in 2002 by Learning Matters Ltd.
Second edition published in 2007.

Library of Congress Control Number: 2013949672

British Library Cataloguing in Publication data
A catalogue record for this book is available from the British Library.

MIX
Paper from responsible sources
FSC
www.fsc.org   FSC™ C013985

ISBN: 978-1-4462-7396-8 (pb)
        978-1-4462-7395-1 (hb)

Contents

1
Introduction

When aspiring Further Education (FE) lecturers come to be interviewed for a place on a programme of initial teacher training, they are often asked the question: 'Why FE? Having decided to be a teacher, why have you chosen this particular sector?' More often than not the answer goes something like this: 'Because the learners want to be there. They have to be at school; but in the post-compulsory sector they're older and they're there because they want to be. I want to teach learners who want to learn. If I was teaching in a school I'd have to be coping with discipline problems, and that's not what I want.' At this point the interviewer will, it's to be hoped, take the opportunity to explain some of the realities of teaching in FE in the twenty-first century.

Yet these candidates' idealism seems based on a sound enough premise. Further Education is not compulsory. Why would learners be there if they didn't want to be? Why should FE not be full of well-motivated learners, willing and even eager to learn? These are questions which are unpacked and addressed in detail in Chapter 2 of this book. Chapter 3 offers an opportunity to look at what some of these learners themselves have to say about their motives and their behaviour, while Chapter 12 explores some of the theories about learner disengagement and ways of addressing it. The remaining chapters look at practical strategies which FE teachers can use in order to motivate learners and to establish parameters of acceptable behaviour.

The intention of this book is to address the immediate needs of the FE teacher by providing advice and ideas of a practical and sometimes pragmatic nature; and also to show where these relate to recent and current learning theory. This is not a theoretical book. It is based very firmly on what teachers and learners in FE have to say about their experiences. It draws on the findings of three research projects into learner behaviour in FE. One focused on the experiences and perceptions of learner teachers new to the sector; one looked at ways in which more experienced teachers defined and managed difficult learner behaviour; and the third focused directly on the learners themselves, and the accounts they gave of their experiences, their behaviour and their motivation. What these teachers and learners have to say can be found in detail in Chapters 3 and 11. Sometimes what they have to say contradicts certain areas of accepted theory and, where this is the case, the reader is encouraged to reflect upon the contradiction in the light of their own practice. The book is by no means claiming that theory is not useful. Rather, it is making the point that, as professionals, we can only judge the worth of theory when we have measured it against our own experience; when it has been, as Keats puts it: 'proved upon our pulses'. As professionals reflecting on our practice we may do our own theorising, and indeed should be encouraged to do so.

The book is designed to meet the needs of the teacher at all stages of their professional development. The content of each chapter in this book can be used for professional development by teachers who are working towards a teaching qualification, and by fully-qualified and experienced teachers whose continuing professional development would benefit from an exploration of issues around learner behaviour and motivation. It presupposes that the teacher, at any stage of their professional development, will find it useful to reflect on their professional practice. It also presupposes that they will have access to support within their institution or place of study, from a mentor, tutor or colleague who can act as a critical friend. This emphasis on reflective practice is in line with the requirements of the Standards. Practical guidance on how to keep a reflective journal in this context and use it as a basis for planning future practice can be found in Wallace (2011). Readers with little prior experience of teaching in the FE sector, or whose experiences have been limited to a narrow range – for example, learner teachers, or teachers on a specialised fractional contract – may find it useful to reflect in their journal on scenarios and dilemmas contained in these chapters, in order to extend the scope of their reflection.

The book uses case studies, dialogue and extracts from teachers' journal entries in order to explore these key issues of learner behaviour and motivation. Taken together, these represent, I hope, an accurate and realistic account of some of the more difficult aspects of the teacher's role. The reader is asked to engage with the material; to analyse and reflect and offer suggestions for future practice. In this sense, too, the book supports the model of the reflective professional.

Chapter 2, as we have already seen, addresses the question of why learner motivation and behaviour have become such an issue in the FE and Training sector. It argues that an understanding of the possible causes which may underlie challenging behaviour will help the teacher to identify effective strategies for dealing with it. In doing so, it seeks to provide a social, historical and theoretical context for the chapters which follow. Some readers may wish to begin with one of the more practical chapters, and turn to the more contextual, theoretical material in Chapter 2 as and when they feel the need to reflect on some of the wider issues which form the background to their classroom practice.

The practical focus of the book begins at Chapter 3, 'Learners talking', which looks at what learners themselves have to say about why they are in post-compulsory education or training and what motivates them to remain there. This is based on one of the research projects mentioned earlier and draws on the responses of learners of all ages and levels of ability. They speak about their previous experiences of education and training and how these have shaped their attitudes. The chapter encourages the reader to analyse and reflect on these accounts, and draw conclusions for their own planning and teaching.

Chapter 4, 'Where do we start?', is about identifying the learner's starting point, and using it. It suggests ways in which the teacher can find and build upon what is positive and also on what simply is. In the process it examines how learners may be motivated by challenging and modifying their often negative construct of 'the teacher'. Chapter 5, 'The Rule Book', looks at establishing rules for appropriate behaviour in order that learning may take place. It suggests ways in which appropriate behaviour can be agreed and monitored, and it examines the disadvantages of having too many or too few rules, or of enforcing them too rigidly.

Chapter 6, 'Great expectations', is about how our expectations of our learners, and their own expectations of themselves, can influence their ability and willingness to learn. It suggests ways in which the teacher can raise their self-esteem and help them to set positive, achievable goals. Chapter 7, 'Breaking out', encourages teachers to think outside the box. It illustrates and discusses the usefulness and limitations of various theories of learning in relation to motivating learners and encouraging positive behaviour, and encourages teachers to recognise and evaluate their own personal theories of learning.

Chapters 8 and 9 look at older and younger learners respectively, exploring the skills and strategies necessary for working with adult returners and with 14–16 year-olds engaging with a vocational curriculum as an alternative to school.

Chapter 10, 'Putting the flags out', looks at ways teachers can help learners to recognise their own achievements, however small. It is about finding successes to celebrate, providing a positive role model, and giving positive and constructive feedback even in the most difficult circumstances. Chapter 11, 'Teachers talking', relates in teachers' own words some of the most difficult or confrontational incidents they have had to deal with. It draws on the research mentioned earlier into the responses of one hundred FE teachers. The strategies they have used are analysed and evaluated in order to present the reader with a range of possible solutions to difficult situations. Chapter 12 provides an overview of some of the theories currently used to explain or address problems of behaviour and lack of motivation among some learners in the sector. It picks up some of the explanations offered in Chapter 2 and unpicks these debates with detailed references.

At the ends of Chapters 3–11 you'll find a set of branching options which offer you a choice of tasks where the emphasis is on reflection, analysis or research. This is intended as an opportunity for you to explore some of the professional values and subject-specific issues which are of particular significance to your current professional development. Some readers may find it useful to work through two, or even all three, of these options.

There are recurring themes which run through all these chapters. They include strategies for appearing confident and in control; ways to counter learner preconceptions about 'The Teacher'; and methods of establishing workable parameters of acceptable behaviour. The main argument of this book is that learner motivation and appropriate behaviour are prerequisites for effective teaching and learning, and that to address either of these issues we have to know something about our learners. Getting to know about the learning needs of those we teach, raising motivation and establishing parameters of appropriate behaviour: the chapters which follow aim to help the teacher to feel more confident about all three of these key aspects of their role.

REFERENCES AND FURTHER READING REFERENCES AND FURTHER READING

Wallace, S. (2011) *Teaching, Tutoring and Training in the Lifelong Learning Sector*, 4th edition. Exeter: Learning Matters.

2
Why are they here? The issues of learner motivation and behaviour in the FE sector

Boredom is just 'What's the use?' in disguise.
Julia Cameron, 1994

The objectives of this chapter

This chapter addresses the question of why learner motivation and behaviour have become such an issue in post-compulsory education and training (PCET) over the last decade. It argues that this cannot be attributed simply to standards of teaching, and that the causes must lie largely outside the classroom. In setting out this argument it seeks to provide a social, philosophical and theoretical context for the chapters which follow.

Introduction: choosing to be in post-compulsory education or training

As we saw in the introduction, there is an assumption among many new recruits to the teaching profession in FE that the learners they will encounter in colleges and other training organisations will be willing and enthusiastic learners. The expression often used is that learners in post-compulsory education and training (PCET) 'are there because they want to be there'. This is a perfectly reasonable assumption to make, of course, since we are talking here about a sector which is 'post-compulsory'. No-one is forced to be there. Therefore every learner enrolled at the college will be there out of choice. Won't they?

Well, of course, many of them will, and many of them will be a delight to teach. They are there because they want to learn and they have found that learning is rewarding, either because it leads to the qualifications they need, or as an end in itself. However, a surprising number of learners will not be like this; they will appear uninterested, uncommitted, even resentful; they will arrive late for lessons, or not at all; they will not complete coursework unless endlessly chased up about it, and sometimes not even then. They will be challenging, confrontational, disengaged and unmotivated; they will send and receive phone calls and text messages in class; they'll wander about the classroom or workshop disturbing those who are working; they'll use offensive language; and worse.

All of this may sound extreme or exaggerated; but anyone who has taught in PCET recently will recognise some of these learner behaviours as part of the FE teacher's everyday experience. To teachers new to the sector, however, this comes as something of a shock. Of 41 trainee FE teachers questioned about their experience of sitting in on FE classes for the first time, every single one reported in their reflective journal that they had witnessed learner behaviour of this kind (Wallace, 2002 and 2013). We'll go on to look at some of their responses to it as this chapter progresses.

But why should such lack of motivation and such challenging behaviour be so prevalent in the sector when, as we have said, learners only enter post-compulsory education out of choice? I think the answer lies with that very word 'choice'. It's a slippery word, by which I mean that it may be used or understood in a way that does not quite reflect its real meaning. If we look back over the final decade of the twentieth century and the first years of the twenty-first, we'll find the word 'choice' used a great deal in the debates over education and training. In 1995, Gillian Shephard, then Secretary of State for Education, told cabinet colleagues:

> We must emphasise the words that people find attractive, such as standards, discipline, and choice. [my emphasis]

Unfortunately, when this was quoted in *The Guardian* (15.9.95, p. 6), a misprint caused the list of desirable words to read, 'standards, discipline, and chaos'. As well as causing us to smile, this misprint may also make us stop and think. It may even nudge us into considering the ways in which the language we use about education and training has begun to dislocate some words from their original sense. How much real choice do learners have at the end of their Year 11 in school? Or, to look at it another way, how many of them have a real choice at all? And might some categories of learners perhaps have rather less choice than others? So when we hear the word 'choice' used in the context of post-16 education, or what we should perhaps now call post-14 education, we should also remember Lewis Carroll's Humpty Dumpty, who declared that 'A word means just what I choose it to mean' (*Alice Through the Looking Glass*, Chapter 6). If 'choice' might sometimes actually mean 'not very much choice at all', then perhaps we can begin to understand why chaos occasionally occurs in some classrooms.

We shouldn't assume, therefore that negative learner attitude and lack of learner motivation in FE are necessarily caused by poor standards of teaching. Certainly it often falls to the individual teacher to come up with ways of dealing with the symptoms of this malaise – and that's why this book has been written. But that is not the same thing as saying that there's something wrong with current standards of teaching nor that 'fixing' the standard of teaching in FE will at the same time 'fix' this malaise. However, understanding the range of reasons behind some learners' unwillingness to cooperate may make it easier for us, as teachers, to find more effective ways to encourage and support their learning.

Lack of choice about being there at all is just one possible cause of confrontational learner behaviour, and one that we shall examine more closely in the following pages of this chapter. But there are other possible explanations, too, which we will need to consider. Since Socrates, philosophers have been asking themselves this question: 'Why do human beings behave badly?' In more recent times, sociologists have begun to ask – and offer answers to – the same question. And psychologists, some of whose ideas will be illustrated in the chapters which follow, have come up with theories about what might motivate or demotivate us or drive us to behave aggressively. There is, therefore, a huge literature on these issues of behaviour and motivation. But in a practical sense it is only of value to us if it works; that is, if we can draw on our understanding of it in order to be more effective in teaching and supporting the learning of our learners. This chapter takes the opportunity to present some of these ideas from sociology, philosophy and psychology in order to establish where our starting point might be. When we are considering how best to motivate a learner or to manage their behaviour, it helps us enormously to have an idea of the possible reasons *why* they are behaving in this or that particular way. The learner will not always be able to tell us; the reasons may not always be easy to articulate; but having some possible reasons in mind will help us to avoid falling into the trap of adopting a deficiency model of the learner. This term – deficiency model – is an important one for us, as teachers, to watch out for. What it means, in our current context, is that learners behave in that way because there is something wrong with them, something lacking; in other words, that they are somehow deficient. We have to watch out for it because it represents a rather lazy way out. We can recognise it in ideas such as 'That learner is just a bad learner. There's nothing I can do about it.' In moments when our confidence as teachers is flagging, we might find we are applying the deficiency model to ourselves, and telling ourselves that the learners are badly behaved and unmotivated because we are somehow deficient as a teacher. It is a central argument of this book that a deficiency model of learners (or teachers) is rarely helpful as an explanation, particularly when our aim is to raise motivation or standards of behaviour. Other explanations can be helpful, however, in providing a context for our interaction with learners, and it is some of these we shall proceed to look at now.

At the same time as we are considering these issues, however, we must not lose sight of the fact that our classes will also include many able and well-motivated learners who have made an informed choice to undertake their current programme of learning. Teaching in FE is an enjoyable, challenging and rewarding experience. If it were not, why would so many dedicated teachers choose this sector? In focusing on the problems and seeking for answers and solutions, we must not allow ourselves to demonise the sector nor stereotype its learners. We should also remember that not all 'difficult' learners are 16-year-olds. Plenty of adults can exhibit challenging behaviour, as we shall see in the chapters which follow, and particularly Chapter 8.

Demotivated by lack of choice

We all know from our own experience that a feeling of control over our own lives – a feeling that we have some degree of choice about what we do – is necessary for our sense of well-being; without it we may easily begin to feel discouraged and disengaged. And so in this respect Gillian Shephard is right, of course. We do like the word 'choice', particularly when we are thinking about our education or that of our children. Ball (1993), however, analyses the contradiction around the word 'choice', arguing that recent policies may restrict rather than extend the choice of learners and parents because, in effect, the power of choice – that is, which learners or pupils go where – often lies now with the institution rather than with the individual. Schools will usually choose which learners stay on to continue their education in the Sixth Form, for example. So let's consider for a moment exactly how much choice the 14- or the 16-year-old who enters FE actually has.

At the end of their Year 11 in compulsory education, the choice faced by most 16-year-olds is whether to stay on at school or to continue their education and training in a Sixth Form College or College of FE. Employment is simply not a realistic option any longer for this age group; and even schemes such as Apprenticeships involve some element of college attendance. So, does the learner stay on at school or go to college? Or does she drop out altogether, thus becoming ineligible for any financial support? Assuming she does not drop out, then how does she make her choice between school and college? In Chapter 3 we'll read some explanations from learners themselves about how they came to enter FE, and why. To judge by these, some of those who enter FE make that choice based on their unwillingness or ineligibility to stay on at school rather than on their preference for FE or for a particular curriculum area. With some exceptions, the underlying principle seems to be this: that learners who don't like school, or haven't succeeded at school, or both, will choose to continue their education or training in FE. Learners who feel comfortable in school will stay on there if the school's curriculum provides the subjects they wish to study. And if the school chooses to have them, of course.

There are two factors operating here. One is that young people who would in the past have chosen to go into employment now may find that their only option, apart from staying on at school, is to go into FE. This is one of the consequences of widening participation. If we widen participation without addressing motivation, we end up with a lot of participants who aren't necessarily enthusiastic or willing. Moreover, learners who choose FE rather than school because they didn't enjoy or succeed at school will include those whose experiences of the education system have taught them to resist and fear it. These particular learners could be in your FE class because they disliked school, not because they wanted to be in FE.

How do we restore these learners' sense of agency? How do we give them back some degree of choice? There are several suggestions in the chapters which follow, including strategies for negotiation and confidence building.

Vocational courses: giving learners a sense of purpose

If learners are enrolling in FE because they were not encouraged by their school to enter the Sixth Form, their achievement at Key Stage 4 is likely to have been discouraging. If this is the case, their choice of FE programme will be limited to those at level 2 or below. Such 'vocational' courses, despite the name, are not likely to lead immediately to employment. Most learners will have to undertake further study or training at level 3 in order to gain a qualification which will begin to open employers' doors. Learners getting their first taste of FE at the age of 14 – that is, at the beginning of Key Stage 4 – will inevitably include many whose performance in National Curriculum subjects has, for a variety of reasons, been disappointing. Sadly, both of these routes into FE can result in learners who do not find education rewarding in itself being recruited onto vocational courses with no very great hope of entry to that vocation at the end of it. This again helps us to understand why they can often appear unmotivated, and why their disappointment and frustration sometimes spills over into unacceptable and challenging behaviour. It remains for us as teachers, then, to give them some sense of purpose; to help them to plan for longer term goals and find ways to help them recognise that there is a reward to be gained in the process of learning itself.

Motivation and the employer-led curriculum

Some have argued, however, that this last point itself presents us with a real difficulty, and that it's the dominance of the work-related qualifications system and its very nature which may be making the FE curriculum less rewarding and less stimulating for younger learners. Of course, the curriculum of FE has always been a predominantly vocational one; but it is sometimes argued that the instrumental, competence-based structures of the vocational qualifications framework, which have been introduced relatively recently, have had the effect of reducing learning to repetitions and rehearsals of work-related tasks and skills. Because many youngsters expect to find the workplace routine mundane and unenjoyable, they respond with the same lack of enthusiasm to the simulated workplace tasks of vocational courses. And added to this, it is argued, there seems to be an acceptance implicit within our current post-16 qualification system that education or training are not rewarding in themselves, but that it is only the qualification at the end that counts. We shall be examining this argument in more detail in Chapter 12.

This is a particularly interesting theory to consider since the white paper, *Extending Opportunities, Raising Standards* (DfES, 2002) presented the argument that young people disenchanted with school would be better motivated if given access to work-based courses and real work environments. If this proves anything it is that for every theory there is a counter-theory! For us as teachers, however, it is a reminder to think of ways in which we can make learning more gratifying – more enjoyable as an end in itself – and less dependent on the idea of simply mirroring the workplace.

The status of vocational education and training and learners' self-esteem

We all know from our own experience, as well as from our reading, that our level of self-esteem plays a key role in determining our behaviour and our degree of motivation. There is – and we shall explore in this section, and further in Chapter 12, how it has arisen – a perception of FE as somehow being a second-best option. It is quite clear, and again we shall hear this from learners themselves in Chapter 3, that there exists a cynicism amongst some learners about what FE is for. We have seen how some might view the sector as simply an extension of their compulsory schooling or, at best a holding station. This idea of post-16 education and training as a means of providing temporary occupation for those who will find no place in the workforce is not a new one. It was an accusation aimed at the youth training schemes of the 1980s (Finn, 1987) as well as at the policies for increased participation of the late 1990s (Ainley and Bailey, 1997). Such a commonly held and frequently expressed idea is bound to have some impact on the motivation of learners, and particularly on the motivation of those who are in FE by default, rather than by choice.

There is another significant factor, too, which arises from the fact that the FE curriculum is a predominantly vocational one. This one is largely historical, and it has to do with status. Despite efforts to establish 'parity of esteem', a vocational curriculum is still widely viewed as somehow inferior to an academic one. This is a view which will inevitably have an impact on the vocational learner or trainee's self-esteem.

It is perhaps of particular relevance at this point in the twenty-first century when, following the 14–19 Education and Skills White Paper (DfES 2005), the decision was confirmed to open up FE provision to 14–16 year-olds. This age-group, which had hitherto been accommodated within compulsory education and engaged in working to the National Curriculum, is now being offered a 'vocational alternative' as part of their timetable in the declared belief that this will improve their motivation and increase their commitment to learning. Whether or not this strategy is working is still open to question.

The Foster Report (Foster et al 2005) and the White Paper which followed it (DfES 2006: *Further Education Reform: Raising Skills, Improving Life Chances*) set out to define the role and purpose of Further Education as one of skills training. It is interesting to reflect on what sort of impact this will have on the status of the sector in the long term.

Linking motivation and behaviour

As teachers we find ourselves dealing not with huge driving forces such as national policies and attitudes, but with their consequences for the individual learner. And it's at the level of the individual that we have to develop our strategies to encourage and support learning. The practical purpose of investigating some of the reasons why a lack of enthusiasm seems to be endemic among certain groups of our learners is primarily to draw some conclusions about what teachers can and cannot expect to do about it. The argument so far in this chapter could be accused of making two broad assumptions. One is that bad or challenging behaviour can always be attributed to lack of motivation; and the other is that both can always be attributed to historical or social factors. In fact, it would be foolish to assume that both of these are always the case. People's behaviour – good or bad – is unlikely to be entirely socially conditioned. As Midgley (2001) points out, this would be like thinking of bad behaviour

> *as a set of peculiar behaviour-patterns belonging only to people with a distinctive history, people wearing, as it were, black hats like those which identify the villains in cowboy films.* (p. 4)

The reality is far more complicated than this. Not all learners respond to the circumstances of their post-16 education and training by adopting a negative attitude or by losing all enthusiasm. And there is no doubt that learners, like the rest of us, must take responsibility for their own behaviour.

There are other useful theories, of course, besides the social and historical ones, as to why individuals behave in ways which we might describe as 'uncooperative' or 'bad' or 'aggressive'. Such theories apply generally, and are not specific to FE learners as some of the socio-historical ones are. They are, nevertheless, useful for us as teachers to bear in mind; and you will find them informing many of the ideas and suggestions in the chapters which follow and considered in detail in Chapter 12. They include, for example, the theory that earlier experiences may set a pattern for our future behaviour; and that lack of self-worth may be directed outwards as anger against others (Freud). And that the feeling of being unvalued, or a fear of mockery, will both act as barriers to cooperation and learning (Rogers, Maslow). Or that hurt inflicted previously during our education may make us fearful of all teachers (Behaviourists). Or that post-modernism and the loss of absolute values have encouraged the belief that good and bad are merely relative and that there is no particular merit in being good (Rorty, 1989). And, on a more mundane level, there are the populist theories which blame bad behaviour on too much television or too little discipline in schools.

The teacher's role

The root causes of challenging behaviour, then, whether they be social, philosophical or psychological, are not simple pedagogical issues susceptible to being tackled on a classroom by classroom basis. So what *can* the teacher do? Well, to begin with, by acknowledging what they can't change, they will be clearer about what they can. Where the promise of an extrinsic reward (for example a job on successful completion of a course) would be viewed with cynicism by the learners, the teacher can try to develop in the learners an intrinsic motivation – an enjoyment of, and satisfaction in, what they are doing for its own sake. Where the learner's past experiences have disinclined them to cooperate now with teachers, we can offer them a more positive model of the teacher–learner relationship. Or where the learner can gain little self-esteem from the nature of the course they are pursuing, the teacher can find other, positive ways to help them to feel good about themselves, both as a learner and as a member of a group.

The 41 trainee FE teachers mentioned at the beginning of this chapter recorded in their reflective journals the experience of their first encounters with learners who were unmotivated and uncooperative. At first they expressed shock and dismay at finding that there are so many learners who behave in this way. For example, one writes:

I observed three different classes today, taught by three different teachers. None of the learners seem to be able to listen to anything for more than about two minutes. Hardly anyone arrives on time. They all start asking to leave on some pretext or the other well before the end. They don't stay in their seats. They shout across the classroom. And they moan at the teacher all the time. In one class one girl kept triggering the ring tone of her phone – a sort of jingle version of the Dam Busters. The teacher pointed out that it was stopping other learners from working. He asked her if she'd do that when her family was trying to watch TV. She said, really belligerently, 'Yeah? So?'

But as they begin to see that this sort of behaviour is happening in a wide range of classes and is being experienced by a wide range of teachers, they begin to explore the idea that it cannot necessarily be laid at the door of bad teaching, nor blamed on a particular 'type' of learner. They begin, in fact, to articulate explanations that do not depend on deficit models of the teacher or the learner, but which draw on the sort of social, political and economic structures which we have been exploring in this chapter.

I'm beginning to wonder if it's overly optimistic to expect enthusiasm from learners. What's in it for them, after all? Just being here at all for some of them means that they're second best. And what are they going to get out of it? A job? I doubt it – certainly not immediately. An interesting course of study? I suppose it could be. But it's so geared to work – it must just rub it in all the time that most of their chances of getting decent work in this vocational area are pretty minimal.

The trainee lecturers' journals highlighted another issue, too. We could refer to this as the retention problem. One of them expressed it like this:

The tutors I observed today tended largely to ignore the background talking that went on in their classes. Some control was attempted, but it wasn't really sustained. One of the tutors said afterwards, when I asked her, that she doesn't feel there's much she can do about it. If she was more heavy handed, things would get confrontational. And also she's got to avoid learners dropping out, because this would mean a loss of on programme funding, and it wouldn't please the college management. So she's just got to tolerate the bad manners. But surely this behaviour must get in the way of the learners learning anything. So what are they here for?

Because funding is contingent on learner numbers – however current policy happens to calculate it – the exclusion or expulsion of learners from courses and programmes of learning carries a financial cost to the college. Inevitably this may lead to situations where unacceptable behaviour is tolerated and carries no dire consequences for the learner concerned. In other words, there may, in extreme cases, be no particular expectation of learners learning.

Other accounts of what is happening in FE

Of course, the snapshots we get of what is happening in FE classrooms and workshops from these teachers' journals cannot tell us the whole story. Some of the current literature on FE presents the situation quite differently. It was argued at one time, for example, that linking colleges' funding not only to learner retention but also to learner achievement would result not so much in the retention of disruptive or disengaged learners as our journal-keepers suggest, but rather in a drive by colleges to only recruit more able learners (Brean and Purcell, 2000). And not all researchers report a sense of disenchantment or a lack of motivation on the part of FE learners. There is also evidence from some researchers that the *general* vocational curriculum, at least in the form of the old GNVQs, actually encouraged and enhanced learner achievement and motivation rather than discouraged it. You will find detailed accounts of these arguments in Chapter 12, with full references to original sources. It is interesting and worthwhile from a professional point of view to read such accounts and to weigh them against your own experience. This is one of the purposes for which a reflective journal is useful. Our continuing professional development as teachers depends not only on our ability to reflect upon our own practice and experience, but also to compare this with the research and theorising of others; to consider how our own developing theory about our role, purpose and practices compares to the wider picture and the currently accepted view of what is happening in the sector.

Conclusion

One trainee teacher wrote in her journal:

> *Some lecturers don't seem to expect anything of their learners at all. One lecturer said to me, just be pleased if they turn up. You'll never get any work out of them. There's not much point trying. You just have to turn up and try to stop them running riot. We're just baby sitters, really. That's what he said. But that can't be right.*

She is absolutely correct, isn't she? That can't be right. As professionals, our prime responsibility is to support learning, and so avoidance of the problem by simply 'babysitting' difficult classes should not be an option we'd want to consider. The purpose of this book is to suggest other options and to equip the teacher with a range of strategies for motivating the unmotivated, for managing potentially challenging interactions, and for making the learning experience more comfortable and enjoyable for learners and teacher alike.

A SUMMARY OF KEY POINTS A SUMMARY OF KEY POINTS A SUMMARY OF KEY POINTS

In this chapter we have:

> considered the element of 'choice' in learners' decisions to enter post-compulsory education and training, and how this might impact on their motivation;

> discussed the role of the vocational curriculum in relation to learner self-esteem, motivation and behaviour;

> explored the links between motivation and behaviour;

> discussed the impact this has on the teacher's role.

REFERENCES AND FURTHER READING REFERENCES AND FURTHER READING

Ainley, P. and Bailey, B. (1997) *The Business of Learning: Staff and Learner Experiences of FE in the 1990s*. London: Cassell.

Ball, S. (1993) Education markets, choice, and social class: the market as a class strategy in the UK and the USA. *British Journal of Sociology of Education*, 4 (1), pp. 3–19.

Brean, S. and Purcell, M. (2000) Get them in – but keep them in. *The Lecturer*, February 2000, p. 11.

DES (1991) *Education and Training for the 21st Century*. London: HMSO.

DfES (2002) *Extending Opportunities, Raising Standards: (White Paper 14–19)* London: HMSO (or www.dfes.gov.uk).

DfES (2005) *14–19 Education and Skills*. Norwich: TSO.

DfES (2006) *Further Education: Raising Skills, Improving Life Chances*. Norwich: TSO.

Finn, D. (1987) *Training Without Jobs*. Basingstoke: Macmillan.

Foster, A. et al (2005) *Realising the Potential: A Review of the Future Role of Further Education Colleges*. Annesley: DfES.

Midgley, M. (2001) *Wickedness*. London: Routledge Classics.

Rorty, R. (1989) *Contingency, Irony and Solidarity*. Cambridge: Cambridge University Press.

Wallace, S. (2002) No good surprises: intending lecturers' preconceptions and initial experiences of further education. *British Educational Research Journal*, 28 (1), pp. 79–93.

Wallace, S. (2013) When you're smiling: exploring how teachers motivate and engage learners in the Further Education sector. *Journal of Further and Higher Education*.

3
Learners talking

It is the province of knowledge to speak and it is the privilege of wisdom to listen.

O. W. Holmes, 1872

The objectives of this chapter

This chapter looks at what learners themselves have to say about why they are in post-compulsory education or training, and what motivates them to remain there. They speak about their previous experiences of education and training and how these have shaped their attitudes. There are opportunities for you to analyse and reflect upon these accounts and to identify ways in which what these learners say could be used to inform your own teaching and planning.

Introduction: personal experiences

This chapter is based on the accounts which real learners have given of their experiences and perceptions of post-compulsory education and training (PCET), and how they came to be there. In Chapter 2 we looked at a number of possible explanations of why so many learners currently in PCET seem to be uncooperative or poorly motivated. This sort of theorising always has its place, not least because it is useful for giving us an overview and for gaining some perspective on how our own role as teachers fits into this equation. Taken on its own, though, it will always seem a little distant from the practicalities of our day-to-day teaching until we have looked at it in terms of specific learner experience. That is why we need to listen, before we go any further, to what learners themselves have to say. We can't really know what being a learner feels like until we hear the learners' own accounts of their experience. As later chapters will go on to argue, we can understand best how to motivate others and encourage cooperation if we are able to imagine ourselves for a moment in their shoes.

There is surprisingly little literature, academic or otherwise, which presents the FE sector from the learner's point of view. Two notable exceptions are Ainley and Bailey (1997), who devote a section of their book to learners' experiences of PCET; and Ball, et al (2000) who present detailed case studies of young people's post-16 experiences. Ainley and Bailey's sample of learners seem on the whole to be reasonably well motivated, and amenable towards the idea of continuing their education and training. Ball et al provide an insight into the social and economic factors which shape the choices made at 16, and argue that, in effect, these aren't really 'choices' at all. You may find that either or both of these provide a useful background to the arguments of the previous chapter and to the learner accounts which are presented here.

This chapter, then, is based on what learners themselves had to say about their experiences of being in a college of FE and what led them there. The learners are drawn from a wide range of age-groups and backgrounds, and from every level of programme from Basic Skills training to HNCs. The examples presented here of what they have to say are chosen as both representative and illustrative of the main issues which emerged from the accounts as a whole. The learners' names and some background details have, of course, been fictionalised in order to maintain their anonymity.

Lester and Kylie

Read through the case study below. What general points would you want to make about this learner's motivation and trajectory?

Lester

Lester is in his first year and is studying three A levels: Sociology, History and Law. His ambition is to go on to Higher Education and get a Law degree which he'll then use to train as a solicitor. Here's what he says:

Lester: *I didn't do that well at school. Nobody expected me to do that well. And I didn't. They wouldn't let me stay to take A levels at school. They thought I was a waste of time.*

Interviewer: *Why do you think that was?*

Lester: *Because of my ethnic group. They just think, oh well, he'll end up driving a taxi or something. Being on the dole or something. So they couldn't be bothered. That's what I think, anyway. But it's different here [FE College]. They treat you different. There's more respect. It's like you're independent. It's like you're an adult. And the teachers are all more relaxed. They talk to you like you're all people — not teacher and learners but just all people, all working together.*

Interviewer: *And what about the subjects you're studying? Do you enjoy those?*

Lester: *I do enjoy them, yes. Because I chose them. My dad wanted me to be an engineer. He wanted me to do all sciences. All my family had this thing about me being an engineer. But that wasn't what I wanted to do. I chose what I wanted to do because I knew I'd enjoy it. And I know where I want to go with it, and I'm going to get there. Because it's my life, do you know what I mean?*

Discussion

The first thing that's likely to strike you about this, I think, is that Lester is a perfect illustration of what we all know FE should be about. In a way he represents the ideal – the sort of learner that teachers entering the sector expect to find. Traditionally FE has always been viewed by those who work within it as the sector of the second chance. Learners who did not flourish at school; learners who – it might be said – were failed by their schooling; these were the learners for whom FE provided a second opportunity to discover their potential. And the success of the sector in this respect was always partly attributed to its less formal atmosphere, its more relaxed styles of teacher–learner interaction, and the scope it provided for learners to make their own choices. Lester conforms to this model exactly. Whatever the truth of his assertions about the assumptions made at his school, there is no doubt that he feels he has gained more validation and respect in FE. The work of Peart (2012) suggests that this may be a common pattern, with young men from minority groups finding FE a more inclusive and motivating environment than school.

Such accounts reassure us that FE can still work like this. The question we have to ask ourselves is, why do more learners not feel as Lester does? Part of the answer, of course, may lie in what he has to say about choice.

I do enjoy them, yes. Because I chose them … I chose what I wanted to do because I knew I'd enjoy it.

As we saw in Chapter 2, for many learners their presence in FE does not reflect choice, and nor does it present them with any choices once there. There is also the question of trajectory: having a clear, attainable target in mind clearly plays an important part in Lester's motivation.

And I know where I want to go with it, and I'm going to get there. Because it's my life, do you know what I mean?

Choice and a worthwhile trajectory may be luxuries which not all learners believe are available to them.

TASK TASK TASK **TASK** TASK TASK **TASK** TASK TASK **TASK** TASK TASK

Have a look now at a learner who is the same age as Lester but whose account of FE reads very differently. As you read through it, make a note of those factors which seem to have contributed to the different perception of the sector.

Kylie

Kylie also did not do particularly well at school. None of her GCSEs were above grade E. She has come to college to retake four of these.

Kylie   *Why did I come to this college? This particular one? It's near my house, isn't it. Why a college? Because I had to retake my GCSEs. If I haven't got them I can't do anything, can I?*

Interviewer *How are you enjoying it?*

Kylie   *Childcare's alright. It's easy. I quite like that. That's my best one. I hate Sociology. It's rubbish. The teacher's stupid. You can't even talk to her. She's just like, 'Shut up and get on with it.' And I'm like, 'If that's the way you feel about it— ' You know? She can stick it. Nobody likes her. We just don't turn up. There used to be about 20 of us. Hardly anybody goes now. What's the point of it, anyway? Even if I got it, what am I going to do? I'll never get my maths. You can't get a job without maths. Not a proper job anyway.*

Discussion

Something that's immediately apparent here is the narrowness of the parameters within which Kylie feels she can make her choices. The way she sees it, she *had* to retake GCSEs to stand any chance of further progression. To do this she *had* to go to an FE college. Now that she's there she *has* to do maths because, 'You can't get a job without maths. Not a proper job anyway.' But she doesn't feel she has much hope of getting her maths, so the question that must be springing to her mind all the time is, *Why is she there at all?* She's there to get the GCSEs that will allow her to progress; but she isn't (according to her) going to get them. And so we have a perfect recipe here for demotivation and disengagement. From where we stand we know she could have chosen an alternative level 2 programme. We can see that she should have been offered more constructive careers advice somewhere along the line. But our knowing that doesn't help Kylie at the point at which she currently finds herself. Her predicament illustrates for us how easily that second chance which the FE sector offers can fail to materialise.

There's another factor in her account, too, which will draw our particular attention as teachers.

I hate Sociology. It's rubbish. The teacher's stupid. You can't even talk to her. She's just like, 'Shut up and get on with it.'

Sociology teachers need take no offence here! This could have been any subject at all. The general point is that learners will not usually enjoy the subject if they don't like the teacher. There are a number of ways in which we might understand that word, 'like', as we shall see in the chapters which follow. It is not necessarily about warm, fuzzy feelings; it can even be something which is better expressed as a wary respect. And there are many reasons why a learner might dislike a teacher. In Kylie's case the problem seems to be that she finds the teacher unapproachable and unsympathetic. What we might take from this is that it behoves us always to give due emphasis to the teacher–learner relationship. When this relationship is working positively, it constitutes one of our most powerful means of raising learner motivation. For Kylie – who knows? – it could have made all the difference to how she felt about herself and her future prospects.

Tony and Aaron

The next two learners are older than Lester and Kylie. They fall into the category of Adult Learners. Both of them are classed as having learning difficulties. Their names are Tony and Aaron.

TASK TASK **TASK** TASK **TASK** TASK **TASK** TASK **TASK** TASK **TASK** TASK **TASK**

Read through Aaron's and Tony's accounts of their FE experience and identify the factors which seem to contribute (a) to these students' motivation; and (b) to triggering inappropriate behaviour.

Aaron

Aaron is in his early twenties and was diagnosed at school as having moderate learning difficulties. He has been a learner in FE for over six years. On first leaving school he attended a Basic Skills programme in order to improve his communication skills. He then enrolled on a regional Intermediate programme of Land-based Studies. From this he has progressed to an NVQ 1 in Horticulture.

Aaron: *I do it because that's what I like. My mum said, 'Go on, then. It's time we had a gardener in the family.' Because she thinks it's about gardening.*

Interviewer: *What do you like best about it?*

Aaron: *I like doing things. I like it when we have to do things and we go out and we really do it. I don't like it when we have to read stuff or just watch stuff. That's when I mess about. I don't like it when we just have to listen. I don't like writing the lists because they go too quick and I can't do that so I don't like it. I just mess about. And I don't like Mr [X] because he shouts at you and he makes you stay out when it's raining and you get soaked. I like doing computers. And I like it when it's just like a few of you – just a few of you and the teacher. Or just me and the teacher because then he helps me.*

Interviewer: *So do you enjoy college, then?*

Aaron: *It's cool, yeah. Everybody here's my friends. And so are the teachers an' all.*

Tony

Tony is in his thirties and has left the army after a head injury which has affected his speech and his short-term memory. He enrolled at the college on the recommendation of his neurologist, as part of his recovery programme. Initially he found himself placed on a Life Skills programme for learners with moderate to severe learning difficulties. He didn't feel this was appropriate to his particular needs, and the frustration he felt over this resulted in some episodes of aggressive behaviour. He is now on a personalised learning support programme.

Tony: *I can't remember stuff. I have to keep learning it. I can't remember. I do it, and then they say to me, 'We did this last week.' And it scares me. Sometimes there's words and I can't – you know. There's things I'm meaning to say but it's like there isn't a word. And they're looking at me, you know? They're thinking I'm thick. But I'm not thick. It gets me – you know – I just go ballistic. It's all in here, you know?*

Interviewer: *What's your goal at the moment?*

Tony: *Get the memory back.*

Interviewer: *And is college helping you with this, do you think?*

Tony: *Well, nothing else is, is it? It's down to me in the end. It's down to me to show them I'm not stupid. If I can't do that, I might as well jack it in now.*

Discussion

One of the most useful things about Aaron's account is that he expresses so clearly what motivates him and what causes him to 'mess about'. The bottom line is that he is motivated by those activities he enjoys, and switched off by those he finds boring or too difficult. Now, this might seem so obvious as to be hardly worth saying; but it raises some interesting issues. A learner might also be switched off, after all, by activities they find too easy. It's not enough, then, to say that we can best motivate learners by only making demands of them that are well within their reach. What Aaron's account more accurately illustrates is the importance of making the learning experience as free as possible from anxiety. Aaron isn't motivated by tasks he fears he'll fail at. He isn't motivated by being shouted at, and he has no enthusiasm for lessons which involve physical discomfort. He also has a preferred style of learning, which is to be actively engaged rather than be a passive recipient. When he is actively engaged he does not 'mess about'. Given the numbers of learners we teach, we don't always make the connection between learner behaviour and a particular style of learning activity. However, this will almost always repay careful attention when it comes to planning and evaluating lessons.

We see the concept of choice raised here, too. Aaron is quite clear about the fact that the subject and occupation he is pursuing is one which he has chosen himself because it's something he enjoys. This sense of having made a genuine choice is something that he shares with Lester; and it is probably no coincidence that both these learners declare themselves to be well-motivated and happy with the FE experience. There's one more factor, too, that Aaron's very clear about, and that is that being in FE involves being among friends. In counting the teachers (as well as fellow learners) as friends, Aaron provides another illustration of the important role that the teacher–learner relationship plays in learner motivation.

Tony's account raises rather different, but equally important issues. In his case the issue of motivation is perhaps a little more complicated. Attendance at college is tied up with his determination to recover. In this respect he seems to be experiencing very little sense of choice here. FE is for him not so much a second chance as an only chance – in his case, of recovering his old self. Indeed, his account is a reminder to us, if we need one, of how important the learner's sense of self is as a factor affecting their behaviour and motivation. Tony feels he has been put in the wrong category; that his innate ability and his previous achievements have somehow been discounted and devalued. Frustration at this has made him behave badly and it has also, in undermining his self-esteem, served to discourage and demotivate him. There is a lesson for us here about the need to acknowledge learners' existing abilities and achievements, whatever they may be. If we fail to do this we will find we are operating exclusively within the deficit model of the learner. That is, we will see only what the learner is still lacking in terms of knowledge, attitude and skills. We won't see the whole learner, and we will miss the opportunity to build on their sense of self-worth, which is vital to effective learning.

Rina and Sara

The next two learners we'll hear from are both adult returners who have enrolled on demanding courses despite their earlier negative experiences of education. Rina is on an Access to HE course. Sara is studying for an HNC in Fashion and Design. As you read through what they have to say below, note down any general issues as well as any which you believe are particularly important to our understanding of adult returners' needs and expectations.

Rina

I did really badly at school, me. I didn't even get put in for some of the GCSEs. They thought it was a waste of time. They didn't like me very much, I don't think, the teachers. They couldn't be bothered with me. When I did something stupid they used to get the other kids laughing at me. So I suppose I knew I was rubbish, really. And when I finished at sixteen I had a few jobs working in shops and that, and then I got married. I was only eighteen when I got married, and I had a family and that. Two kids. And I kept thinking, I ought to go back and do something. But I daren't, you know? I didn't want that whole thing of feeling like I was no good at it – like I was thick. And also I felt like really I should be looking after the kiddies. Or I should at least be earning something so I can buy them stuff. I still feel like that, really. I still feel guilty about the kids. It took me ten years to come back, and I was terrified. Even now I don't really believe I'm going to get anywhere. I still have days when I think the teachers don't like me. I'm sure they think – you know – 'Oh it's her. She's just thick.' Or they laugh about me. Laugh about me wanting to go to university. Like, 'In your dreams.'

Sara

I was a right tearaway at school. I was, honest! I used to get teased when I was little because I was so good and I was a bit of a boff. But once you started playing the teachers up – that was how you made friends. You were either in with the teachers and you had no friends, or you gave the teachers a hard time and then you were really popular. That's how it was at our school. And in the end I was a natural at it. I wouldn't let anybody tell me what to do. I was horrible! I bet they were right pleased when I left. I was only sixteen, but I started working in a bar. I worked in a few bars, but I never really did a proper job. I was messing about like that for nearly eight years. And then I started going out with Rich and he said why didn't I go and do some proper qualifications and get a proper job. And I thought, yeah, I can do that. But I was that scared. It was like if I went back they'd start trying to boss me about again. They'd start trying to tell me what to do. And also there was the money. I've still got a bar job in the evenings – unbelievable! And sometimes I'm rushing round, you know, and I don't get my college work done properly because I've got to get to work. Or I'm working late and I get into College all tired and ratty and I start giving the teachers a hard time. It's easy to slip back into it, that's the trouble. When you've been like that you see a teacher and it sort of sets you off. Even though you know they're really nice people. It's funny, that.

Discussion

What Rina and Sara illustrate all too well is the fact that FE learners come to us carrying all the baggage of their previous educational experience. In the case of adult returners, that can be very heavy baggage indeed. The implications for us, as teachers, can be quite daunting. Both Rina and Sara have a very negative memory of teachers – Rina because she believes hers thought her stupid (and, whether the picture she paints of them is accurate or not, the important point is how she now feels about it).

> *They didn't like me very much, I don't think, the teachers. They couldn't be bothered with me. When I did something stupid they used to get the other kids laughing at me.*

And Sara because they represented an authority she had decided to rebel against.

> *It was like if I went back they'd start trying to boss me about again. They'd start trying to tell me what to do.*

What happens, then, when learners like Rina and Sara come into FE, is that they bring this impression of teachers with them, and it becomes our task to establish a more constructive model for them of what a teacher does and is. The aggression and resistance we can sometimes encounter from learners may in reality be directed at some teacher or teachers who upset them or left them feeling negative about themselves a long time ago. This is important for us to bear in mind if we are not to turn such encounters into trench warfare.

In terms of issues which are pertinent to adult returners in particular, what we are reminded of here in Rina's and Sara's accounts is that the lives of adult returners to FE are complicated. As well as all the other baggage, they often have family responsibilities, conflicting priorities, financial commitments, a sense of guilt at taking time away from the children, their partners, their domestic responsibilities. This can affect their motivation and mood, as well as their capacity to give their full attention to their college work.

> *And sometimes I'm rushing round, you know, and I don't get my college work done properly because I've got to get to work. Or I'm working late and I get into College all tired and ratty and I start giving the teachers a hard time.*

In other words, the adult learner we see in our class may be only the tip of the iceberg. There may be a multiplicity of roles and responsibilities which we never see, but which will impact upon the way the learner relates to us and to their learning.

Lee, Abdul, Deb, Gaz, Richie, Jo, Brendan

For our remaining examples, let's go back to some 16- and 17-year-old learners. When we talk about motivation and behaviour in FE this is usually the age group we have in mind as presenting us with the greatest challenge. We'll have a look, therefore, at what some of them have to say about us, their teachers. Some of this may make for uncomfortable reading – but it's nothing we can't handle!

TASK TASK TASK **TASK** TASK TASK **TASK** TASK TASK **TASK** TASK TASK

As you go through this section, you should consider:

- **What can we learn from these learners' accounts about the qualities in a teacher they seem to respond well to?**

- **What behaviours or qualities in their teachers seem to have the effect of discouraging, demotivating or antagonising them?**

Lee

[Teacher X], she's great. She's a good laugh. She makes it funny. And you can tell she's enjoying herself. Teachers always give up with me, but she just won't give up. And you can't, like, rattle her cage. She never shouts or nothing. She has this look, you know. This look – and then the next minute she's laughing again. So I turn up for her lessons. They're alright.

Abdul

It's like he can't be bothered. He doesn't want to be there. You can tell he doesn't want to be there. Well that's alright, innit? Because we don't want to be there either.

Deb

I was really surprised when he said, 'Call me [X].' I didn't think you call teachers by their first name. You never call teachers by their first name at school. But it's like he wants to be a person, like you're two people and feel like you can talk to him. And if you don't do the work or something, he doesn't get mad, he gets worried about you. And he says, 'Is everything alright?' and stuff like that. So you know he's really bothered. So you don't get scared about handing stuff in to him because you know he's not going to get mad with you if it's rubbish.

Gaz

He's just pathetic. He never looks at you. We just do what we want. Half the time he looks like he's scared, and half the time he shouts. Completely loses it. It's well funny. His face goes all red and that. Nobody takes any notice of what he says. He hates us and we don't give a — about him.

Richie

She really knows what she's talking about. That's the thing about her. And she likes it, you know? And that makes you like it as well. Because it's interesting. And she listens to you. Like, when you answer a question or something, she listens to you like she's really interested. And if you get it wrong or something, it doesn't matter, you know? She's like, 'Well that's an interesting way of looking at it, Richie.' And she's like, 'Good try.' And all like that. You feel like she's really pleased with you, know what I mean? That's why I go.

Jo

Even the teachers think it's boring. Like there's this one teacher and she says, 'Right, we've got to do this thing this morning and I know it's boring and that, but we've got to do it.' And you think, well, if even the teacher thinks it's boring, what's the point? I'd rather be having a laugh and that.

Brendan

He makes you work. He doesn't shout or nothing. He just looks at you. You can have a laugh with him though. He never disrespects you or nothing. And we don't disrespect him. His lessons are alright.

Discussion

So, first of all, what behaviours or qualities in their teachers seem to have the effect of discouraging, demotivating or antagonising these learners? Perhaps we could summarise them like this.

- **Lack of enthusiasm:** 'It's like he can't be bothered.'
- **Lack of commitment:** 'He doesn't want to be there.'
- **Shows no interest in the learners:** 'He never looks at you.'
- **Lack of self-confidence:** 'Half the time he looks like he's scared.'
- **Lack of assertiveness:** 'We just do what we want.'
- **Loss of temper:** 'Half the time he shouts. Completely loses it.'
- **Hostility:** 'He hates us.'
- **No interest in the subject:** 'I know it's boring and that, but we've got to do it.'

This makes rather dismal reading. We can reassure ourselves with the knowledge that there are very few teachers who conform to this model. They simply wouldn't survive, for one thing. But there's one important purpose this list serves, and that is to confirm that what we do as teachers does make a difference. However heavily social and economic factors may impact on learners' behaviour and motivation, what we do and the way we relate towards our learners can have considerable impact too.

Now, on a more positive note, what can we learn from these learners' accounts about the qualities in a teacher they seem to respond well to?

The list you came up with here probably looked something like this.

- **Sense of humour:** 'She's a good laugh. She makes it funny.'
- **Enthusiasm:** 'And you can tell she's enjoying herself.'
- **Commitment:** 'She just won't give up.'
- **Assertiveness:** 'She has this look, you know.'
- **Openness and approachability:** 'But it's like he wants to be a person, like you're two people and feel like you can talk to him.'
- **Care and empathy:** 'He doesn't get mad, he gets worried about you.'
- **Sound knowledge of the subject:** 'She really knows what she's talking about.'
- **Acceptance and encouragement:** 'She listens to you like she's really interested.'
- **Personal impact:** 'He makes you work. He doesn't shout or nothing. He just looks at you.'
- **Respect for learners:** 'He never disrespects you or nothing. And we don't disrespect him. His lessons are alright.'

These, then, are the qualities or attributes in the teacher which are, according to these accounts, most likely to motivate learners and encourage manageable behaviour.

They look like a tall order; and it may be that none of us can quite live up to all of them all of the time. But if one of your colleagues is suffering from flagging energy on a particular day, for example, you can step in with the energy for two! Elsewhere I have written about the 'Best Teacher' (Wallace, 2011). The qualities and attributes we have just been considering are the ones most often cited when people are asked to define 'best teacher' in terms of their own experience of learning. In the chapters that follow we shall see some examples of what happens when this model of teaching is applied to motivating learners and managing their behaviour; and we shall also see some examples of what happens when it is not.

A SUMMARY OF KEY POINTS A SUMMARY OF KEY POINTS A SUMMARY OF KEY POINTS

In this chapter we have:

> considered what learners have to say about their experiences of education and training;

> discussed the nature of 'choice', and how it impacts on learners' motivation;

> explored the impact that learners' previous experiences may have on their current attitudes to learning;

> considered the specific needs of adult learners;

> extrapolated from learners' stories a list of the qualities in a teacher to which they respond most positively.

Branching options

The following three options are designed to provide you with additional opportunities for reflection, analysis and research. You may choose the option which best supports your currently identified needs, as set out, for example, in your action plan for a teaching qualification or for your continuing professional development (CPD). Alternatively, you may choose to work through two or even all three tasks.

1. *Reflection*
   - How much do you know about your learners' previous experiences and about their aspirations, particularly with relation to your own specialist subject? What examples of specific learners can you think of?
   - Do you know sufficient to enable you to take their experiences into account in your planning and teaching?
   - If so, what examples can you think of which illustrate how you have done this? And if not, what activities could you introduce into your lessons which would enable your learners to tell you more about themselves?

2. *Analysis*
   - Look at your most recent lesson plan. Which aspects of it demonstrate that you are taking your learners' previous experiences and current fears and aspirations into account? Are there opportunities for you to be more responsive? If not, why not? Are there any factors about your specialist subject which would make this easier or more difficult?
   - Take one group of learners and consider to what extent their previous achievements and/or behaviour (e.g. in school) are an accurate predictor of their current performance and/or behaviour.

3. *Research*
   - Using the internet or available library facilities, look at what is currently being written about learner attitudes and behaviour in the FE sector, and particularly – if possible – in your own subject area. One of the best sources for this are academic journals. You might start your search in journals such as *Research in Post-Compulsory Education*, or the *Journal of Vocational Education*, or the *British Educational Research Journal*. If you find access to these difficult, look in the educational press for reports of current research.
   - To what extent are the themes and concerns identified in this research also apparent in the learner attitudes and behaviour within your own organisation?

REFERENCES AND FURTHER READING REFERENCES AND FURTHER READING

Ainley, P. and Bailey, B. (1997) *The Business of Learning: Staff and Learner Experiences of FE in the 1990s*. London: Cassell.

Ball, S., Maguire, M. and Macrae, S. (2000) *Choice, Pathways and Transitions Post-16*. London: Routledge-Falmer.

Peart, S. (2012) *Making Education Work: How Black Men and Boys Navigate the Further Education Sector*. London: Trentham.

Wallace, S. (2011) *Teaching, Tutoring and Training in the Lifelong Learning Sector*, 4th edition. Exeter: Learning Matters.

4
Where do we start?

'Begin at the beginning,' the King said, gravely,
'and go on till you come to the end: then stop.'
Lewis Carroll, 1865

The objectives of this chapter

This chapter is about the importance of identifying the learner's starting point, and using this to inform your teaching and planning. It will help you to discover what is positive and how to build on it; and how you can address learners' behaviour by challenging and modifying their construct of the 'teacher'.

Introduction: the importance of communication

We began the practical chapters of this book by looking at what learners have to say about their learning. There is good reason why this was the appropriate place to begin. Our starting point – if we want to motivate and engage our learners – should always be the learners themselves, whether we are planning our teaching or reflecting on our practice. Understanding the needs and attitudes which the learner brings to the classroom or the workshop is an essential first step in establishing a positive learning environment. It is, it could be argued, more important in the first instance than translating the syllabus or course specifications into a scheme of work. If the scheme of work you've designed is incompatible with your learners' need for constant reassurance or active learning or note-taking skills, for example, it's unlikely to be particularly effective in achieving the required learning outcomes.

Hearing what learners have to say, however, is not always straightforward. In the previous chapter we heard from learners who were willing and able to express their views and their feelings about what motivated them and what didn't; and how their previous experiences of learning had affected their current needs. When learners are able to do this, and we are able to listen and hear, we have a useful basis on which to build, both in terms of our professional relationship with them, and the way in which we structure their learning. However, not all our learners will communicate such information to us so easily; or they may communicate it in ways which are not immediately evident; ways which may seem more like a challenge than an attempt at communication.

Andy

Let's have a look at one of Andy's classes. Andy is working towards his initial teaching qualification. As part of his course requirement his teaching of this class is being video-taped, so that he can review it and write a self-evaluation. His tutor is also present, sitting at the back of the class, to write a formal report on his teaching. It is an English Language class. There are twelve learners, six male and six female, all aged between 16 and 19. This is only the third lesson he has had with them. Here is what the video camera sees:

The tables are arranged in a horseshoe, and Andy starts by sitting on the teacher's table at the front of the class and briefing the learners on the task they're about to do. They'll each be given a picture on which to base a piece of descriptive writing. There is silence as he speaks. Most of the learners appear to be listening. One or two are making notes.

Andy then gives out the pictures, one to each learner, as he walks around the inside of the horseshoe of tables. As he does so, he checks with each of them that they understand the task and that they have paper and pens with them. The learners are cooperative, even enthusiastic – nodding, asking questions, picking up their pictures and looking at them with interest. Then he comes to a young woman – Nicola – who responds very differently. She doesn't look at him. She doesn't respond to him. When he sets a picture down for her on her desk she simply folds her arms on the table in front of her and lowers her head down on to them as though she was going to sleep. Andy hovers there for a moment or two, looking uncertain; but then moves on to the last two learners, who respond positively like the others. He goes back to the front of the class, asks whether or not there are any questions and, receiving no response, tells them to begin the task, for which they have twenty minutes.

As the learners work, he moves around the room, inside the horseshoe, giving help and asking questions. The first time he approaches Nicola's table she sees him coming and starts packing her things away, putting her pencil case and folder back into her bag and pushing the picture away from her to the far side of the desk. Then she puts her head down on her arms again. Andy hunkers down so that he's not looming over her, and says, 'Come on, Nicola. Let's see what you've written.'

No movement. No response.

'Come on. What's the matter? Don't you like the picture?'

No response

'Do you want another picture?'

Still no response.

Andy waits a moment, stands up, glances towards his tutor, and then moves off to help other learners.

The second time Andy approaches her table, Nicola, still head down, begins slowly tapping her forehead against her table – not hard, but audibly, nevertheless. She hasn't looked at her picture. Her pens and folder are still in her bag. Andy hunkers down again. He says: 'Come on, Nicola. What are you doing?'

No response.

'Come on. Don't do that. You'll hurt yourself.'

No response. Andy looks uncertainly towards his tutor. Then he says:

'Come on, Nicola. Let's have a look at that picture. Let's see what we want to say about it.'

No response.

Andy remains there a moment or two, then stands up and moves on to the next learner, who is working well and who, like the others, responds to him in a friendly way.

When the twenty minutes for the task are almost up and Andy has almost completed his third circuit of the room, he approaches Nicola again. This time, as she sees him coming, she begins banging her forehead more forcibly against her desk. Bang. Bang. Bang. Andy stops in his tracks and, raising his voice above the murmur of on-task noise, he says: 'OK. Time's up. You've all worked very hard. Let's take a ten minute break. Back in here at quarter past.'

The learners, who hadn't been expecting a break, file out happily, chatting. Nicola goes with them, leaving behind her bag and her coat just like the rest of them. Andy looks over towards his tutor, frowning. And the camera switches off.

TASK TASK TASK **TASK** TASK TASK **TASK** TASK TASK **TASK** TASK TASK

Take some time to read this account through again, and consider the following questions:

- **How would you feel if you were the teacher and this was happening to you?**

- **What would you have done in these circumstances?**

- **Do you notice anything on the second reading that you missed on the first – anything that might help you to interpret what was happening here?**

Discussion

It's important to reflect about how you would feel in this situation, because the way we feel affects the sort of decisions we make. What's happening here is an example of learner behaviour which seems to be escalating out of control. It begins as non-engagement or non-cooperation, but quickly becomes something more than that. If it were simply 'bad' behaviour, such as shouting, swearing, refusing to settle down, we would at least have models in mind of how to deal with it – even if they weren't very effective models. The problem here is that we're being challenged by behaviour for which we don't have a ready-made strategy. This is likely to leave us feeling some degree of apprehension, or even panic. And of course, when we're in the grip of such a feeling, we're less likely to think clearly, and less likely to make sound decisions. This is why classroom situations such as the one Andy finds himself in are so challenging for the teacher. It's obvious that a decision has to be made, that some action has to be quickly taken. But what's the right one?

So, would you have called a break at this juncture? It's a tricky question, particularly if a mid-session break is in contravention of college rules. As you reflect on what you would have done, you may like to discuss your ideas with a colleague or mentor, or record your thinking in your reflective journal.

A couple of points which become more evident on second reading are, firstly, that Nicola was 'acting up'. That is, she was aiming her behaviour at Andy, making sure that he was approaching and could see clearly what she was doing before beginning to bang her forehead on the table, for example. Secondly, she seems to intend coming back into the class after the break. Both of these points are likely to have bearing on how we begin to interpret her behaviour.

Reflective journal
14 October

Well, I wasn't looking forward to that lesson, with a camera there <u>and</u> my tutor. Weird thing was, what I was worried about was that the students wouldn't be able to settle because of the camera – that they'd play about or clam up. But I think because it was set up in the back corner, there was only really me who was aware of it once the lesson got going. And then I forgot about it as well because I found myself completely thrown by Nicola T's bizarre behaviour. It was like a bad dream. Here was this class, looking all interested and working well, and then suddenly there's Nicola acting more and more oddly. It just got worse. First she looked bored. Then she started banging her head on the table! And then she started banging it really hard – and I thought, '—! What's she going to do next? Pick the table up and throw it at somebody? Leap out the window?' So I called a break. I couldn't think what else to do. She just wasn't responding to anything I said.

The thing is, I found I spent the whole time, the whole lesson, focusing my thoughts on that one student. And there were 11 others, all working really hard, all deserving my attention, all deserving lots of positive feedback and praise. And I couldn't think about anything except how do I stop Nicola cracking her skull against that table. Now, that can't be right, can it? And what's worse, I don't even know what the matter was. Did she find the task too hard? Was there something about the picture I gave her that upset her? Or was it something that had gone wrong at home? Boyfriend trouble? Violence? I don't know. How am I supposed to know if she won't tell me? Complete mystery to me. At least when she came back after the break she didn't do any more head banging. Just put her head down and went to sleep. Thank goodness for small mercies.

Let's look now at what Andy has to say about how this situation made him feel, and how he initially interprets Nicola's behaviour.

Discussion

We can probably all empathise with what Andy was feeling here. He sums up very well the dilemma of the teacher who finds him/herself in this situation.

I have all these learners deserving of my time and energy; and yet all my attention is taken up by this one learner.

He goes straight to the heart of things here. The teacher's prime purpose is to facilitate and support learning. Anything which detracts from this must be addressed and resolved. What this means for us in practice is that we can't deal in the long run with situations like this simply by ignoring the difficult learner. Even if her behaviour is not distracting other learners from their learning, it is certainly telling us that she herself is not engaged nor on task. We see here how Andy is at a loss to interpret Nicola's behaviour; but he is absolutely right to assume that it is saying something. It is saying something about how she feels and why. It's a form of communication, albeit an oblique and very troublesome one. It is often useful to bear this in mind when confronted by challenging behaviour. We can't always hope to understand what it's saying. But it's saying something.

Let's see now how Andy's tutor unpacks and explains this in a little more detail when she writes up her observation for Andy to read.

Observation of Practical Teaching

Date:	14 October
Subject:	English Language
Number of Students:	12

Planning and resources

Your introduction to the lesson was clear, and you briefed the students well for the task, allowing them plenty of time to ask questions and seek clarification. The task itself was appropriate – both interesting and challenging – and you'd chosen some interesting pictures to use. I like the way you moved from student to student, engaging with them one-to-one while they were working, and asking just the right questions to encourage them and move them forward.

▶

Communication and quality of learning

It appeared to me that you get on well with these students. You seem to have established a good relationship with them, and they're prepared to work hard for you. You should give yourself credit for this. You deserve it. I say this because I imagine that what is preoccupying you at the moment is the problem with Nicola. Please don't lose sight of the fact that for most of your students this was an enjoyable and productive learning experience; and you'll see this, I'm sure, when you get around to watching the video.

Points to consider for future practice

You told me immediately after the lesson that you didn't think you'd handled the problem with Nicola very well. I think the difficulty here is that we have to have some idea what the problem might be before we can make any sensible decision about how to handle it. One thing which was clear to me, as an observer, was that Nicola was aiming these histrionics at you. She wasn't just generally expressing how she felt; she wanted to communicate this specifically to you – escalating the dramatic behaviour whenever you were looking at her. My guess is that she wanted you to ask her what was wrong. She'd probably have said, 'Nothing' – until you'd asked her a sufficient number of times; but she wouldn't have worked so hard at showing you how she felt unless she wanted this question posing somehow, in some form: 'What's wrong?'

Perhaps the answer's simply that she thought the proposed task was too easy, and wanted you to know she felt bored. But there's always the possibility, of course, that it's something far more serious than that – something which it would be more appropriate for her to discuss with a student counsellor rather than with her teacher. That's why I think you were correct not to push her for an answer in the middle of the lesson. I also think, given the alarming way her behaviour was escalating, that you were right to call a break. This was a good way to defuse things – let some steam out of the pressure cooker. It needn't have been a fully-fledged coffee break, however. Just an, 'OK. Have a couple of minutes to take a break, have a chat, stand up to stretch your legs a bit.' That sort of thing. Under cover of the chatter you might have been able to get Nicola to give you some indication of what the matter was.

As the situation stands, you know Nicola has a problem, but you don't know what it is. I think the best course would be to ask your section head if she'll have a word with her. Although Nicola is clearly targeting you and seems to want you to ask what's wrong, this could just potentially put you in a difficult or embarrassing situation as a young male teacher. Whatever her problem, she chose to remain in your class. She could easily have escaped at the break if just being there was so unbearable. She preferred to carry on performing her drama to you. That's why I think this situation needs handling with care.

CLOSE FOCUS CLOSE FOCUS CLOSE FOCUS CLOSE FOCUS CLOSE FOCUS **CLOSE FOCUS**

Do you think the tutor has made a fair assessment of the situation? Is there anything here you would challenge? You may like to discuss this with a colleague or mentor, or use these questions as a starting point for recording your thoughts in your reflective journal.

Discussion

We began by talking about starting points. One way of expressing this is the need to know where our learners are 'coming from'. Andy's plight illustrates this perfectly; and these are some of the things we can learn from it.

- Challenging behaviour is a form of communication. It tells us the learner is experiencing a problem, even if it doesn't tell us what that problem is.
- We can't begin to help a learner to learn until we know where she's coming from.
- When considering a learner's starting point we shouldn't be thinking of it only in terms of their current knowledge and skills, but also in terms of their level of motivation, their state of mind, and their prior experience of learning.
- The challenging behaviour of just one learner can affect our ability as teachers to give sufficient support and attention to the other learners in our class.
- It is our professional responsibility, therefore, to seek some solution, although this does not necessarily mean we must solve the problem ourselves.

Understanding learners' attitudes

Knowing where our learners are coming from can often mean having to take into account their prior experience of learning. Teaching in FE, we are going to encounter learners who, as a minimum, have already spent eleven years in the education system; some of them may have spent even longer. Their attitudes towards education will already have been formed. And by the very nature of FE – sometimes thought of as the sector of the second chance – many of these learners' experiences of education will not have been positive ones. That is to say, they will perhaps not have experienced the pleasure of success, or have received very much praise, or have gained much self-esteem from their prior experiences of learning. Moreover, they may have formed a construct of 'the teacher' which is not a particularly positive one.

Just as every teacher and aspiring teacher will have a personal ideal – a construct of 'the perfect teacher' based on their own best experiences of being taught (Wallace, 2011), so too will every learner have an idea that pops into his or her head at the sound of that word: 'teacher'. Sadly, in many cases, this idea will carry associations of oppression, of a control that's resented. It may trigger memories of being criticised or thwarted, or simply being made to do something they didn't want to do, either because it didn't interest them or it was beyond their abilities and left them open to ridicule. The learner's construct of 'the teacher' is very powerful. As you stand in front of a class for the first time, happily assuming that these learners are seeing you – a perfectly pleasant and caring professional whose intention is to help them learn and to enjoy themselves in the process – what some learners may be seeing is something completely different. Imagine it as though a cinema projector was superimposing upon your pleasant and friendly features the threatening face, sewn together Frankenstein style, of all the teachers who, however unwittingly, have made these learners feel bad about themselves and resistant to learning.

Discussion

You'll know whether this barrier exists from your learner's attitude. The clue is usually when your own positive approach and best efforts meet with rudeness, aggression, non-cooperation. As for what to do about it, the first rule is:

Don't take it personally

Admittedly, this is far more easily said than done. But it helps if you keep in mind that this is, in all probability, not about you at all, but about how this learner has come to feel about 'being taught'.

As for how you begin to deal with it – well, this is an attitude that has built up in the learner over several years, and so it is unlikely that you'll solve it in a moment. Given our analysis of the problem, it's clear that one answer must lie in getting the learner to revise his or her notion of 'the teacher' – from someone who makes them feel bad about themselves to someone who helps them build their self-esteem and sense of achievement. This will take time; and, of course, in the face of persistently challenging behaviour, it's by no means an easy thing to do.

Why not just use strict rules and punishments? Wouldn't this be easier? We'll be looking more closely at the idea of Rules in the next chapter; and it's only commonsense that certain rules – agreed parameters of acceptable behaviour – are necessary in any environment where people are working together. However, seeking to adjust learners' behaviour simply through the application of rules and punishment will always have a limited effect. It might or might not prove useful in terms of control; but it will not necessarily be effective in encouraging learning. To become willing and effective learners, people have to feel some degree of intrinsic motivation – motivation that comes from within themselves. Those who are intrinsically motivated are more likely to engage actively with their learning, and to develop into lifelong learners. This will happen because they come to find learning, in some sense, personally rewarding. In simple terms, it makes them feel good. Extrinsic motivation, on the other hand – getting the learner to learn by using threats of punishment or offers of reward – might achieve a short-term behavioural change, but leave untouched the learner's basic attitude towards learning. If we are to produce a society of lifelong learners then it is learners' attitudes that we need to address. If the desire to learn comes from within, then all the rest follows.

The idea of changing learners' attitudes, of helping them to develop an intrinsic motivation to learn, can sound somewhat idealistic, perhaps, given some of our experiences as teachers in the FE sector. However, as we saw in Chapter 2, the possibilities for using extrinsic motivation to encourage learning are becoming more and more limited. We can no longer say with conviction to learners on 'vocational' courses, 'Work hard and there'll be a job at the end.' We know this will not necessarily be true. We can no longer say to the learner with confrontational behaviour, 'Behave, or you'll be out.' The unit of funding he carries will weigh heavily against such a step being endorsed. The reality is that such a carrot and stick approach is increasingly ineffective, even if we wanted to use it.

This brings us back, then, to helping the learner to find their own motivation to learn. We've looked already at two steps we might take towards achieving this.

- **Discover the learner's starting point. Get to know the learner.**
- **Help the learner to revise their negative construct of Learning and The Teacher.**

The next step – setting parameters of acceptable behaviour – will be achieved much more effectively if it follows on from these two. It's a step which we'll look at in some detail in the next chapter. For now, we can summarise the strategy like this:

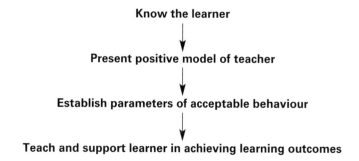

Changing the way learners feel about their learning

So, how do we ensure that learning, whatever it has meant to the learner previously, can now become a positive and rewarding experience? How do we demonstrate that The Teacher can actually be someone who helps them to feel positive about themselves?

Another advantage in getting to know where our learners are starting from is that, as well as discovering something about their attitudes to learning, we can learn something about their individual level of skill and knowledge. There may be things the learner needs to learn before they can begin to address the outcomes specific to their programme of learning. For example, they may need to learn note-taking skills; or they may need to become familiar with the layout of a keyboard. They may need help in mastering certain social skills. Some types of challenging behaviour may arise simply as a result of the learner not knowing what behaviour is appropriate to that particular situation. On the other hand, what they need to learn first may reside purely in the affective domain. They may need to learn to have trust – in you, the teacher, or in their own ability to achieve. Or they may need to learn the pleasure that follows achievement; that learning something new can make them feel good about themselves.

Let's have a look now at how one learner teacher reflects on these issues in her journal after watching an experienced teacher with a class of 14–16 year olds.

---

22 February

My mentor's away ill today. I sat in instead with Gail who was taking a Kick Start class. I have to write 'taking' and not 'teaching' because I couldn't honestly see much teaching and learning going on. At least, not stuff the students were supposed to be learning. They were learning <u>something</u>, I suppose, but it was pretty counter-productive, in my opinion.

Actually, I really thought I was going to learn something in this class because everyone's always going on about how good Gail is at discipline – how she sorts the students out and they daren't give her any trouble. I could do with some of that! But anyway, this is what happened.

►

She was doing some basic psychology with them – a bit ironic, this – and she wanted them working in small groups, so she asked a couple of the girls to push some of the tables together. One of the boys – a little undersized shrimp of a lad who'd been joking about a bit – said something like, 'I'll do that. That's a man's job.' And G. says, really loudly, 'Oh. It's a man's job, is it, Darren? Why's it a man's job?' And this gets the whole class's attention. So they're all smiling and watching what's going to happen. And Darren says, 'Well, because men are stronger aren't they.'

He's obviously trying to get her going, because he stands there grinning round at the class. They're all standing about while these girls move the tables. So anyway, G. goes up to him – right up to him. She must be nearly six foot tall. And she towers over him and she looks down at him and she says, 'Men are bigger and stronger than women, are they Darren? Is that right?'

And all the class roars with laughter. They just fall about. And poor little Darren goes bright red. He tries to brazen it out for a second, but then he laughs lamely and starts looking in his bag. Actually, I wondered if he was going to cry. But he didn't.

I suppose I can see why she doesn't have much trouble with student behaviour. They'll all be pretty wary of her, even though they're laughing along. I don't suppose any of them wants to be next in line for a public humiliation. But this doesn't help me. I don't want to do it like that. I think those students were learning something I don't want mine to learn: that a teacher can pick up on anything you say and use it to humiliate you. She might have shut Darren up, but what's the main thing he's learnt in that lesson? And what's he likely to learn in the next one or the next, feeling how he must now about the teacher?

I don't think it was necessary to slap him down like that. He wasn't interrupting the others' learning. If I'd chosen to make any response to the 'man's job' thing, I'd have picked up on the offer of help – the positive bit – and let him join in with the two girls to shift a desk or two. And then thanked him. It was an opportunity to make him feel good about himself and his ability to be useful in the class – and G. just let that go. She missed it and did the complete opposite instead. But I'm not going to tell her that! I wouldn't dare!

CLOSE FOCUS CLOSE FOCUS CLOSE FOCUS CLOSE FOCUS CLOSE FOCUS **CLOSE FOCUS**

How far do you agree with what this student teacher has to say about Gail's methods?

Do you agree with the journal writer's alternative way of handling the incident?

If you do not agree with her method or with Gail's, explain what your own approach would have been.

You may like to discuss this with your mentor or tutor, or use the questions as the basis for an entry in your reflective journal.

Starting with what is good

This chapter has been about starting points and how to identify them. Where we start from. Where our learners are starting from. In the process we have, perhaps inevitably, focused upon problems: how to identify them and how to resolve them so that we can really get started on teaching and supporting learner learning. Sometimes, however, in getting to know our learners, we discover good places to start, as well as problems to resolve. A good illustration of this is found in the story of *Kes* by Barry Hines. You've probably read the book or seen the film. In this story a teacher of English in a Secondary school is able to use one teenage boy's consuming interest (in this case it is in the kestrel the boy is training) as a source of motivation for engaging with some of his schoolwork. This is an unusual starting point. For other learners it might be their kind of music, or some film or television programme, or a sport, or a particular celebrity which will draw their interest. You might discover that a learner has a particular talent, not obviously related to the subject you are teaching: impersonating someone famous, for example, or a high level of competence and confidence in ICT. These are all starting points. They all represent ways in which learners can be helped to build their self-esteem and to find the experience of learning an enjoyable and non-threatening one.

Another way to start with what is good is to monitor our own attitude towards our learners. This sort of metacognition – awareness of what we are thinking – or metamood – awareness of what we are feeling – is an important attribute for the teacher. If we are feeling fearful or resentful of a learner, or cold and negative towards them, and are not sufficiently conscious of our feelings to conceal them, we may well let them show in our behaviour or our tone of voice, or simply in our body language. And this will serve only to reinforce the learner's preconception that teachers are hostile, that they are an enemy to be confronted. Carl Rogers (1983) counsels that our learners will learn most effectively when they have our 'unconditional positive regard'. This is a tall order. It's not always possible to control how we feel about our learners. But we can cultivate the ability to remain aware of how we feel, so that we can be on our guard against communicating a negative attitude towards a learner, which would discourage them from learning. 'Unconditional positive regard' may seem an impossible ideal. It provides, however, a good starting point, because it reminds us that we can and should behave in such a way as to make all our learners feel valued for who and what they are. We may draw a line at accepting some of their behaviour or attitudes but we should demonstrate that, as individuals, they are all valued, and all valued equally. Not only does this establish a model of acceptable and socially just behaviour, but it also demonstrates to the learner that their negative construct of The Teacher may need re-examining. This is part of a set of values which lies at the heart of our professionalism. In the chapters which follow, we take a pragmatic approach to exploring various ways of putting these values into practice.

A SUMMARY OF KEY POINTS A SUMMARY OF KEY POINTS A SUMMARY OF KEY POINTS

In this chapter we have:

> emphasised the importance of starting with what is 'good';

> explored the importance of correctly interpreting what learners are communicating by their behaviour;

> discussed the dilemma of weighing one learner's demands for attention against the needs of the rest of the class;

> explored the significance of learners' preconceptions of 'The Teacher' and 'Learning', and how these can be addressed;

> discussed the importance of helping the learner to find their own motivation to learn.

Branching options

The following three options are designed to provide you with additional opportunities for reflection, analysis and research. You may choose the option which best supports your currently identified needs, as set out, for example, in your action plan for a teaching qualification or for your continuing professional development (CPD). Alternatively, you may choose to work through two or even all three tasks.

1. *Reflection*
   - Think back to the last occasion you had to address a learner's behaviour. How did you interpret what was going on? What did you assume the learner was 'communicating' to you at the time?
   - Do you think there might be an alternative way of interpreting what was being communicated?
   - How will your subsequent lesson planning or approach change as a result of this interaction? Does your subject specialism make this easy or difficult? If you decide to change nothing, what are your reasons for this decision?

2. *Analysis*
   - Look at your most recent lesson plan. Which aspects of it demonstrate that you are starting from what is 'good'? For example, are you using what you have gleaned about learners' interests or skills to inform your choice of learning activities?
   - Take one group of learners and consider how you can gain some insight into what motivates them, particularly in relation to your subject, and how individual motivation levels differ. How wide is the range of motivators within the group? What proportion of the learners would you judge to be intrinsically motivated? How can you use all this data in your future planning and teaching?

3. *Research*
   - Take ten minutes to conduct some research of your own. Choose one group of learners and find out how they would describe their own attitudes to learning, and particularly to learning your subject. You may find putting them into small focus groups the most effective way of eliciting this sort of information.
   - Then, using the internet or available library facilities, find out how your learners' views compare to those described by other current researchers, either in academic journals or in reports of current research in the educational press.
   - Discuss with a colleague or mentor how you will use all this information to inform your future planning and teaching.

REFERENCES AND FURTHER READING REFERENCES AND FURTHER READING

Rogers, C. (1983) *Freedom to Learn for the 80s*. Columbus, OH: Merrill.

Wallace, S. (2007) *Getting the Buggers Motivated in FE*. London: Continuum.

Wallace, S. (2011) *Teaching, Tutoring and Training in the Lifelong Learning Sector*, 4th edition. Exeter: Learning Matters.

5
The Rule Book

The end of law is, not to abolish and restrain, but to preserve and enlarge freedom.

John Locke, 1690

The objectives of this chapter

This chapter is about establishing rules for appropriate behaviour in order that learning may take place. It suggests ways in which appropriate behaviour can be agreed and monitored; and it examines some of the pitfalls which may follow from having too many rules or from enforcing them too rigidly.

Introduction: general principles

It's impossible to talk to learner teachers about the management of learner behaviour without someone bringing up the issue of rules: what rules we should have in our classroom or our workshop, and how these should be enforced. And this is quite right; we do need to establish clear rules – what are now more commonly called parameters of acceptable behaviour – as part of creating an environment in which our learners can feel safe and motivated to learn. What these parameters should be, and how we set them, will depend very much on the circumstances and on the nature of the learners.

Parveen

In order to arrive at some general principles, let's have a look at some extracts from a reflective journal written by Parveen, who has recently completed her FE teaching qualification, and is now at the beginning of her first full year of teaching.

---

3 October

I've had to take on a Schools Link group of 14- and 15-year-olds for a while because their teacher has gone on sick leave. M. is taking over some of my Key Skills sessions to make room on my timetable for this lot. I say 'this lot' because, having met them this morning, I can't say I'm much looking forward to teaching them. Their other teacher only had them for a couple of weeks, but I think he must have just let them run riot.

There were only four of them waiting outside when I got there. They got the computers on as soon as I'd unlocked the room and let them in. And I thought, oh good – they're keen. I waited a bit for the others to arrive (there are 20 on the register). I suppose I must have waited about 10 minutes; and then I thought I'd better make a start anyway. But I couldn't get these four to turn around and listen to what I was saying. And when I went round to look at what they were doing it was obvious they were just doing their own thing – messing about on the Internet, or playing games. Three more students drifted in, and then another two. The last two didn't even switch their machines on. The boy just started wheeling about the room on his chair (all the computer room chairs are on castors) making silly noises. The other one, the girl, just put her head down on her arms and appeared to go to sleep. I had several goes at getting their attention. I tried clapping my

---

▶

hands. I tried raising my voice. In the end I just switched all the machines off at the main switch, at which point there was a loud groan and yelps of protest from the seven who were logged on. They got quite aggressive. 'What you done that for?' and that sort of thing. I told them I needed them to listen carefully to my instructions before I'd switch back on again; and that if they weren't going to listen to what I had to say they may as well not be there. At this point one of them got up, picked up his bag (he'd never even taken his coat off), and made for the door. I shouted at him, 'Sit back down, now!' And he just stuck his chin out and said, 'Or else what?' and just walked out. I looked at the rest of them and it seemed as though they were all grinning at me, waiting to see what I'd do. All except the sleeping girl, who hadn't even looked up. Then the lad who was skating about on his chair said, 'Can we go for a break, Miss?' And they all took this up. 'We ought to have a break, Miss.' There were only 20 minutes to go before the end of the lesson, and I just thought, why not? It was a relief, really, to let them go.

Yes, it must have been. This can often be one of the difficulties of taking over someone else's class; that the standards of behaviour they expect don't tally with your own. Poor Parveen. But before we have a look at her own reflections about future strategy, let's examine what was happening and see whether we can come up with some strategies of our own.

TASK TASK TASK **TASK** TASK TASK **TASK** TASK TASK **TASK** TASK TASK

Read through the journal extract again and consider:

1. What could Parveen have done differently?

2. What rules would it be useful to establish with this group?

3. How would you prioritise those rules? (For example, if you could establish only one, which one would it be?)

It would be a good idea to jot down your answers, or discuss them with a colleague or mentor, so that you can establish whether you agree or disagree with the ones suggested later in the chapter.

Discussion

1. What could Parveen have done differently?

Let's look first of all at what Parveen herself has to say about this.

4 October

I've been thinking about that awful class I had yesterday, and I've come to the conclusion that I started off all wrong. I shouldn't have waited for the rest of the class to turn up. It gave those first four the chance to start on something I didn't want them doing – and once they'd started, it was hard to stop them. I should have seized their attention before they even sat down, and briefed them on the first task before I switched on the main switch. Then when the next two lots of students arrived late, I could have briefed them as small groups, round my desk, before letting them sit down and switch their machines on. I'm sure that's the answer – to seize control from the first moment, to get the students all on task.

Do you agree? Would this strategy have worked, do you think? What about the learner who put her head down and went to sleep, and the one who was playing about on his chair? Would the strategy Parveen proposes have ensured that these two stayed 'on task'?

It's worth spending a few minutes here to consider the behaviour of these two learners. Anyone who has taught in the FE sector is likely to have come across learner behaviours such as these at some time or another. It would be a mistake, however, to disregard them as inevitable, or even as simply odd. Both of these learners are quite clearly drawing attention to themselves. More, they are drawing attention to the fact that they, for one, aren't intending to do any work in this lesson. What both of them are doing by their behaviour is saying, 'Look! Look at me! I'm not doing this work!' *Now, why would they do that*? If they simply wanted to avoid working, wouldn't it be more advantageous not to draw the teacher's attention? What's going on here?

At the most basic level, we'd probably be safe in assuming that the main thing differentiating these two learners from the other seven is that they don't want to work on the computers. The others, although they're ignoring the teacher and the set task, seem relatively interested, competent and confident as far as computers are concerned. It would be wise, therefore, for the teacher to consider the possibility that the behaviour of the two off-task learners is an attempt to draw her attention because they need her help. This will not necessarily be true in every instance – rules of thumb are rarely that reliable – but it is always worth consideration. The chair boy may be avoiding sitting at the keyboard because his classmates will tease him if it becomes apparent he's no expert. It's far better for his image to show a bit of bravado by playing up the teacher. And then it will seem as though he's not working just because he chooses not to, not because he doesn't know how.

Or perhaps the converse is true. Perhaps his computer skills are already so advanced that he's bored by anything this lesson might teach him. In either case, the teacher needs to find out; and the only way to do this is by engaging the learner in dialogue.

Here, however, we might find that commonsense is contradicting theory. We are often told in books on the psychology of education that we shouldn't reward attention-seekers by giving them what they want – that is, attention – since this will only provide positive reinforcement of that particular behaviour. That is, it will encourage the learner to continue behaving in that way because they are learning that to do so gets them what they want; and what they want is attention. The theory is that the learner must learn to ask for help in acceptable ways, rather than by acting disruptively or non-cooperatively. In many situations this would no doubt be sound advice, but the difficulties of applying it in Parveen's class are immediately evident. A pragmatic approach – speaking with the learner and listening to what he has to say in an attempt to discover the reason for his resistance – would seem to be the most sensible way forward. In a chapter about rules, this is a useful one to bear in mind: that educational theory is only useful when it works in practice.

2. What rules would it be useful to establish with this group?

Again, let's look first here at what rules Parveen, after some reflection, decides she should establish.

---

4 October (continued)

One thing's for certain: I'm going to have to impose a bit of order on that class or they're going to make things very difficult for me. They're going to have to learn some ground rules.

(i)   Everyone must arrive on time.

(ii)   Everyone must listen quietly to instructions before starting on the computers.

(iii)   No one must move from their place while the lesson is in progress.

(iv)   No one must speak without putting up their hand.

(v)   No one must shout out.

(vi)   No one to leave the room without my permission.

(vii) No one to be working on anything other than the task I've set them.

(viii) No break (it's only a 50 minute lesson so they don't need one).

They've been getting away with things since the beginning of term. It's time to pull them up. I shall put these rules up on the board at the beginning of the next lesson, and let them know that anyone who breaks them is in trouble.

Goodness! It sounds as though they're not going to know what's hit them. Parveen is clearly determined to sort them out. To what extent does this set of rules match the one that you've drawn up? If Parveen were to ask you, what would be your professional judgement about her list? Like any good teacher, Parveen has two good reasons for wanting to establish the parameters of acceptable behaviour in her classroom. One is that it provides a better learning environment, and the other is that it makes her own task of supporting and encouraging learning easier to carry out and more likely to succeed. It's important, when thinking about 'rules', to always bear these two purposes in mind. If you read that last journal extract again, you'll see that this teacher, in this particular instance, is taking a slightly one-sided view. Perhaps she's still feeling upset about what happened. But look at what she says:

> *I'm going to have to impose a bit of order on that class or they're going to make things very difficult for me.*

and

> *They've been getting away with things since the beginning of term. It's time to pull them up.*

We might think this sounds a little too much as though rules are being devised here as a punitive device; or at the best simply for the benefit of the teacher. Rules produced in this way are less likely to be successful than rules which are designed to support learning. And this leads us on to our next question, which is:

3. How would you prioritise those rules? (For example, if you could establish only one, which one would it be?)

If I had to choose only one rule from Parveen's rather comprehensive list it would be number two:

> *Everyone must listen quietly to instructions before starting on the computers.*

The criterion I would apply in choosing this one would be precisely that which we have just been discussing: the promotion and support of learning. If learners are clear about the learning activity they are engaged in (and assuming that an activity has been chosen which will engage their interest and meet their needs), much of the rest will follow. Disruption is less likely; and, although it may not solve the problem of late arrivals, learners will hopefully not be jostling to get out of the classroom before the end of the lesson.

CLOSE FOCUS CLOSE FOCUS CLOSE FOCUS CLOSE FOCUS CLOSE FOCUS **CLOSE FOCUS**

If this is not the rule you yourself would have prioritised, this doesn't mean that you're wrong and I'm right. What is important, however, is that you are able to give a rationale for your choice, and to explain and justify the criteria on which your decision was based. Your reflective journal is a good place to do this; or you may wish to expound your argument to a colleague or your mentor.

Parveen, meanwhile, is sticking to her eight rules. So let's have a look now at her journal entry for the next week and see how well they worked.

TASK TASK TASK **TASK** TASK TASK **TASK** TASK TASK **TASK** TASK TASK

As you read it through, make a note of what advice you would offer her.

---

10 October

The Schools Link class again in the Computer Room. I made them wait outside this time – and I waited with them – until six of them had arrived, and then I unlocked the room and took them in. They did a lot of grumbling and moaning because I wouldn't switch the machines on until I'd written the rules up on the board. When I'd finished I told them to read them through and tell me if they had any questions. I couldn't get them completely quiet, and I don't know whether they all read them all. The only questions were: 'Are we allowed to breathe?' and 'Can we go now, Miss?' I gave out the sheets with their tasks on – keyboarding exercises to improve their speed – lots of groans from them – and only then did I switch the computers on. It immediately became apparent that no-one was doing the tasks and that they were just messing about. So I switched the machines off again. The boy who was scooting the chair about last week shouted 'Oi, Miss, out of order!' So I drew his attention to the rule about shouting out, and told him he would have to apologise. He said, 'No way.' When I insisted, he grabbed his bag and made for the door, with all the others roaring encouragement. I said, 'Sit back down. The rule is that everyone stays in their place.' – or something like that. I thought for a minute he was going to shove me out of the way, but instead he made this big show of stomping reluctantly back to his seat, playing to the audience. But it didn't feel like a victory to me at all. At least none of the others turned up. Six was just about manageable. But even so, I spent the whole time pulling them up for breaking every one of those rules, constantly having to remind them. It felt even worse than last time.

Discussion

So, what advice would you offer? It would probably include some or all of the following:

- **It may be more productive to discuss and negotiate these kind of rules, rather than to simply impose them.**
- **The more rules you have to enforce, the less time you have for teaching and learning.**
- **One rule may be sufficient, if it's the right one.**
- **Your primary purpose, as a teacher, is to support learning. The parameters you set should bear this in mind. Learners remaining in their places, for example, doesn't necessarily support learner learning in situations where it may be useful for one learner to help another.**
- **Avoid direct confrontation wherever possible. It can cause an already difficult situation to escalate.**

What you will have jotted down, in fact, if you have spent some time over this exercise, is a set of rules about – yes – about making rules! They are guidelines which you can test and apply in the course of your own professional practice. They won't all be applicable, of course, in all situations; and, as your experience broadens, you may wish to amend and add to them.

CLOSE FOCUS CLOSE FOCUS CLOSE FOCUS CLOSE FOCUS CLOSE FOCUS **CLOSE FOCUS**

Let's take the last guideline on that list and look at it a little more closely. We have seen two examples of direct confrontation in Parveen's journal. They both arose over learners leaving the room without permission. The first took place during her initial lesson with the class:

> I told them I needed them to listen carefully to my instructions before I'd switch back on again; and that if they weren't going to listen to what I had to say they may as well not be there. At this point one of them got up, picked up his bag (he'd never even taken his coat off), and made for the door. I shouted at him, 'Sit back down, now!' And he just stuck his chin out and said, 'Or else what?' and just walked out.

In her subsequent journal entries, Parveen doesn't get around to reflecting on what was going on here. So let's analyse it for her.

Question: *She describes herself twice here, speaking to the class and to the individual learner. What is her manner of address*?

Answer: Well, she issues what appears to be an ultimatum to the whole class, which could be interpreted along the lines of, 'Do this or get out' ('if they weren't going to listen to what I had to say they may as well not be there.') When one of the learners takes up the challenge and acts on this, she issues a direct order: 'Sit back down, now!'

Question: *Why was this manner of address – the ultimatum and the direct order – not a good idea under the circumstances*?

Answer: Because they didn't leave her any ground for retreat. This is illustrated very clearly when the departing learner demands to know: 'Or else what?' Or else what, indeed. If the learner is determined to get out of that door, there's very little that the teacher can do about it, within the parameters of her own professional conduct. Ultimata and orders are one way of trying to impose rules. They are not, however, necessarily the best or the only way. And the more rules we draw up, the more we impose upon ourselves the necessity of enforcing them. And there we are, spending far too much time issuing orders and ultimata.

Question: *So how could she have addressed this situation differently? What alternative form of words could she have used*?

Answer: Instead of saying, 'If you're not going to listen to what I have to say, you may as well not be here' she could have said:

- **'Let's have a look at what you should be able to do by the end of this lesson.'**
- **'Is there anyone here who can already do this?'**
- **'I wonder if all this noise means that some of you can do this already? I'd like those who can do this already to team up with someone who's still working on it, and give them a hand.'**
- **'Let's find out from everybody what you'd like to have achieved by the end of this lesson. One at a time.'**

All of these are worth a try. What they have in common is that they open up a dialogue with the learners. The teacher isn't just issuing orders, but is creating the possibility of discovering why the learners are behaving as they are.

Instead of saying, 'Sit back down, now!' she could have said:

- **'James? Where are you going?' (But she would have to have known his name for this, and I suspect that she didn't.)**
- **'Where are you going?' (Notice the difference it makes when the name is missing. Immediately the question sounds more accusatory, less friendly.)**
- **'I'd prefer it if you sat down. There are only a few minutes to go before the end of the lesson.'**
- **'Listen. I'll need to talk to you about why you're leaving early.'**
- **'Come on. Don't leave us. I need your help for this next bit.'**

It may well be that none of these will prevent the learner from leaving if he's determined to go. But all of them will give the correct message without raising the levels of anger and indignation and without creating a situation in which the teacher is seen to be directly disobeyed. And all of these suggestions are likely to be more effective if the learner is addressed directly by name. You can demonstrate this for yourself now by prefixing a learner's name to each of them, and trying both versions. The management of learner behaviour is very much easier when you know your learners' names. This is another rule to add to our list.

Negotiation

If we look at the language Parveen has used up to this point in her journal, we can see that she is operating within the assumption that rules are something which she decides upon, and then enforces by imposing them on the learners. Look at some of the things she says:

I'm going to have to impose a bit of order.

They're going to have to learn some ground rules.

I shall put these rules up on the board at the beginning of the next lesson, and let them know that anyone who breaks them is in trouble.

I spent the whole time pulling them up for breaking every one of those rules.

When William Hazlitt wrote that 'Rules and models destroy genius and art', he was making a serious point which we can extend usefully to education. He was not advocating chaos and anarchy. What he was suggesting was that enthusiasm, creativity and initiative will not easily flourish in a situation where too many externally imposed rules allow only one pre-specified way of doing things. For example, in Parveen's class there may have been learners who already possessed some of the skills she was trying to teach them. If the rule is that they have to go through all this again, they're likely to feel uncooperative and unenthusiastic. If the rule is that they all have to stay in their places, how can the more expert learners use their skills to help their classmates – an activity that might well rekindle their motivation?

We all know that we have to have rules; but they're more likely to be adhered to if we've all agreed to them. Let's see what happens, then, when someone mentions this idea to Parveen and she begins to try it out.

---

17 October

Third lesson with the dreaded group. I've put a lot of thought into what I should do. Yesterday I was talking to our section head about it, and I suddenly found myself getting quite upset. And then she said something really interesting. She said: 'Every single one of those students, if you could talk to them on their own, would admit there's a need for rules. Everyone feels safer if there are rules – as long as they see the sense in them. Why don't you get them involved – get them to suggest some rules?'

I don't think I'd have had the nerve to try this if the idea hadn't come from her. But she said it was quite a normal thing to do and that she always does it as a matter of course when she meets a new class. I think the trouble is I've just been sticking with what I learnt from my mentor last year. He was a bit of a stickler for discipline – which worked OK for him. So anyway, I let them all into the room this morning – there were ten here this time – and I didn't put the machines on, but waited until all the students were sitting down and looking towards me. And then I gave them a great big smile and said, 'OK. What rules would you like to have for this class? What rules would help you to work better?'

After we'd had a few of the inevitable witticisms such as, 'Leave early'; 'Not have to turn up if we don't want to'; 'You're not allowed to give us boring stuff to do'; 'James has to change his pants more often'; they actually began to come up with some sensible suggestions. The ones we agreed on in the end were:

- **No one is allowed to disturb anyone else if they're trying to work.**

- **If someone can already do the task I'm covering, they're allowed to go and help someone else who can't.**

- **If they all get the planned task done, they get to access the Internet until the end of the lesson.**

Next thing I got them to do was to write up these rules, print them out, and put them at the front of their files. We also agreed to have two volunteers each week who would 'police' the rules. I don't know how well this will work in the long run – but the difference it made to today's lesson was amazing. They worked really well and there was a much friendlier atmosphere. I even felt they were beginning to like me.

TASK TASK TASK **TASK** TASK TASK **TASK** TASK **TASK** **TASK** TASK TASK

This sounds like a happy ending. But in fact, of course, it's not. It's a beginning – a new start – and it's by no means certain that Parveen and her class will live happily ever after. But she has taken a step towards getting the learners to engage with their learning. She will no doubt have to take others. There are some indications in this last journal entry (and in the earlier ones, too) as to what some of these might be. Read through the entries again and see whether you can identify at least two issues which Parveen will need to address in her future planning for this class.

Discussion

As far as most of the learners are concerned, their motivation for the subject is not in doubt. They want to work on the computers. We know this because Parveen tells us that 'They did a lot of grumbling and moaning because I wouldn't switch the machines on.'

But they seem very poorly motivated to carry out the tasks which she sets them. The impression that emerges is that they don't find these tasks very interesting. We know this because one of the rules they suggest is that 'You're not allowed to give us boring stuff to do.'

Now, we could argue that this is the equivalent of an aspiring pianist complaining about having to practise their scales: a repetitive but nevertheless essential step in achieving competence. We also know that 'It's boring!' is the eternal lament of the young. However, in this case, we have some evidence which indicates that some of the learners may feel bored simply because they are already familiar with, and able to carry out, the tasks and procedures she is covering in her lesson plans. Otherwise why would they have come up with the rule 'If someone can already do the task I'm covering, they're allowed to go and help someone else who can't?'

One of the issues that Parveen is going to need to address, therefore, is differentiation – setting differentiated tasks and goals appropriate to the individual learners' current needs. She will also need to look at ways to engage learners' enthusiasm for the tasks she sets them. This may involve revising or extending her range of teaching methods, or finding ways to illustrate to the learners the relevance of what they are learning to their own aspirations and goals. This, in turn, will mean getting to know the individual learners, and devising activities which allow her to work with them on a one-to-one basis so that she can engage with them and listen to what they have to say. Agreeing rules with your learners is only the first step. Whether you can continue to work together within those rules will depend on how effectively you plan to meet their needs; and this in turn usually comes down to how well you know your learners. The centrality of the teacher–learner relationship in establishing the positive behaviour of learners is a theme we shall keep coming back to.

Parveen will also have to address the issue of low attendance (only about half of the learners on the register seem to be turning up), and to investigate the needs of the boy in the chair and the sleeping girl.

CLOSE FOCUS CLOSE FOCUS CLOSE FOCUS CLOSE FOCUS CLOSE FOCUS **CLOSE FOCUS**

The final sentence of Parveen's last entry reads:

> I even felt they were beginning to like me.

How important a factor do you consider this to be in the context of setting parameters to student behaviour? This is an issue which you might like to reflect on in your journal.

Implementing the rules of others

The parameters governing behaviour in our classrooms and workshops and other environments in which we teach extend beyond those set by ourselves and our learners. First of all there are the rules and regulations set by the institution in which we work. These will cover behaviour – both that of the learners and our own – and other issues such as health and safety. Some of the regulations may seem comparatively minor. For example, it may be a college rule that no food or drink is allowed in the classroom. Working as you are, in a professional context and within a set of professional values, it is part of your professional responsibility to uphold these rules, *even if you don't personally consider them important*. This also means not trivialising them; not saying for example, 'I know it's a stupid rule, but ...' Or 'If it was up to me I'd let you ... eat your sandwiches off your computer keyboard', or whatever. This is part of what the requirement for teachers to understand agreed codes of practice is about.

Secondly, of course, there is the law of the land. If a learner comes to you and says, 'I need to tell you something. Do you promise not to say anything to anybody?' – beware! You don't have the immunity of a doctor or a priest, who can claim ethical reasons for maintaining confidentiality. If, having extracted a promise of silence from you, a learner tells you he's shot his grandma, you become an accessory after the fact unless you report it to the police. The best response to such a request for confidentiality is to say: 'If there's something you want to talk about, of course I'm willing to listen. But I can't promise to keep it confidential because there may be something in what you tell me which I need to pass on, in your interests or in mine.'

A SUMMARY OF KEY POINTS A SUMMARY OF KEY POINTS A SUMMARY OF KEY POINTS

In this chapter we have:

> **emphasised the importance of knowing your learners, listening to them, and learning their names;**

> **discovered that the test of a rule's usefulness is whether it helps to support learning;**

> **considered the advantages of encouraging learners to take ownership of the rules;**

> **identified the disadvantages of having too many rules;**

> **argued that theory is useful only if it works in practice.**

Branching options

The following three options are designed to provide you with additional opportunities for reflection, analysis and research. You may choose the option which best supports your currently identified needs, as set out, for example, in your action plan for a teaching qualification or for your continuing professional development (CPD). Alternatively, you may choose to work through two or even all three tasks.

1. *Reflection*
   - What rules do you apply in your classroom or workshop? Are they your own, or have they been agreed with learners at the outset? Are any subject-specific? Do the learners themselves take any responsibility for policing the rules?
   - Is there anything about your choice and application of rules that you might want to change, having read this chapter?

2. *Analysis*
   - Think back to your most recent lesson plan. Which rule was most frequently challenged? For example, was it the rule about phones? Or about iPods?
   - Why does the enforcement of this rule prove problematic? Is it anything to do with the subject you teach? Is it to do with the rule itself? (For example, rules about phones run counter to popular youth culture.) Or is it about the manner in which it's applied? (For example, indiscriminately, and involving no consultation with learners.) Or is it something about these particular learners? (For example, they're full of energy and easily distracted.) Or is it about the content or style of the lesson? (For example, it's not very inspiring and so fails to hold their attention.)
   - Is there a different way you could approach this rule, for example by discussing it with learners and building in some opportunity for them to take ownership of it?

3. *Research*
   - How much do you know about the rules of the organisation within which you teach? In addition to the clearly signed rules such as 'No smoking in college buildings', there will also be a whole range of rules and codes of behaviour set down in organisational policy documents, such as the Equality Policy or Anti-Bullying Policy. Find out what policy documents and statements exist, and look through those with which you're not already familiar.
   - How might you draw on this information in the way you address rules in the classroom or workshop? Is there any conflict between the institutional rules and the demands of your specialist subject?

REFERENCES AND FURTHER READING REFERENCES AND FURTHER READING

Rogers, B. (2006) *Classroom Behaviour: A Practical Guide to Effective Teaching, Behaviour Management and Colleague Support*. London: PCP.

Wallace, S. (2007) *Getting the Buggers Motivated in FE*. London: Continuum.

(The first book is about schools, but most of the advice it offers can be usefully applied to post-compulsory education and training.)

6
Great expectations

Possunt, quia posse videntur (They can because they think they can).

Virgil

The objectives of this chapter

This chapter is about how our expectations of our learners – and our learners' expectations of themselves – can influence their willingness and ability to learn. It suggests ways in which these preconceptions can be challenged, and examines strategies for raising learners' self-esteem and helping them to set positive, achievable goals.

Introduction: it's not a battle!

When Nelson sent a signal to his fleet before the Battle of Trafalgar *'England expects that every man will do his duty'*, was he reminding the crews to obey orders – *behave the way you're supposed to, or else* – or was he letting them know that he had absolute faith in their courage and ability; that he and all England knew that these sailors and their officers would do their duty? I prefer to think it was the latter. Shipboard discipline may have been draconian, but in this instance Nelson probably knew that he could get the best out of these people by speaking to them as though they were already heroes. There's something we can learn here, and apply to our own much smaller battles, which are often about gaining learners' attention, getting them to recognise the satisfaction to be gained from learning and achieving, and convincing them that there's more reward in learning than there is in disruption and challenging behaviour. Our battles can sometimes even be with ourselves when, for instance, we have to go in there and face a class whose behaviour we feel has slipped beyond our control.

We are using the metaphor of a battle here because that's sometimes what it can feel like when we're trying to motivate learners and manage their behaviour. However, it's a metaphor we should beware of internalising as a model for our professional practice! Teaching and supporting learning is not, and should not be, a battle between the teacher and the learners. The trouble is, it can sometimes feel like one. This is probably because so many of our learners do seem to see it this way; in Chapter 5 we saw how Parveen, when she began drawing up rules for learner behaviour, was also in a sense drawing up battle lines, which only made her task even more difficult.

Gloria

Let's have a look at another teacher now. Gloria is on a part-time contract, teaching Health and Social Care. This is her first year of teaching, and she has just begun working towards her teaching qualification. She's already teaching ten hours a week when she receives a call from her college asking if she will also come in and take over a Communication class for a few weeks. Having agreed to do this, she reflects on what happens next in the journal she's keeping as part of her teacher training programme.

TASK TASK TASK **TASK** TASK TASK **TASK** TASK TASK **TASK** TASK TASK

Read through the journal entry below and consider the following questions:

1. **At what point, if any, during this scenario could Gloria have taken steps to improve her situation?**

2. **What, specifically, was she frightened of? What's the worst that could happen?**

3. **How would you interpret the learner behaviour that Gloria saw as she entered the room? What do you think this behaviour is communicating?**

4. **What are the possible reasons for the learners feeling like this?**

---

3 December – midnight

Can't sleep. Decided to write this up – try to decide whether I'm getting it all out of proportion. I said I'd take over the class, partly for the experience, and partly because I want to appear willing, in case a full-time post comes up. All I knew was that they were Construction trainees, thirteen of them, all male, and the person who normally taught them Communications was off sick. The class was on the top floor of J Block, four flights up. I was walking up the stairs with the register and the work sheets when I passed the Section Head of Construction coming down. He said, as he walked past me: 'Have you come in to do the Communication Skills? They're all up there waiting for you. Complete waste of time, and they know it is. I won't tell you what they did to the last bloke. Won't be seeing him again. I hope you last a bit longer. Doubt it, though.'

I suddenly felt frightened. My heart started banging away, and it wasn't just those stairs. I was thinking, 'Oh no. Have I brought the right sort of work for them? What's going to happen when I walk in? What if they make me look stupid as soon as I walk in – how am I going to spend the next hour and a half with them? What did they do to their last teacher? Oh no. *What did they do to their last teacher?*'

When I came to the bottom of the last flight of stairs, I could hear them. They were laughing and shouting and swearing. And I just wanted to drop the register and run. When I got to the top of that last flight I knew I should stop for a minute and get my breath back so that I didn't go in there all red in the face and breathless. But I also knew that if I hesitated for one moment, I wouldn't be able to make myself do it. I'd just turn and run. So I pushed open the door and went in. Twelve big lads lounging about at three rows of tables, bags slung everywhere, some on the tables being used as pillows, some on the floor. One lad standing on the windowsill rattling at the top window. When I stepped into the room and stopped, some of them noticed right away and shouted out to the others who were still yelling and laughing. 'Ay-up, lads. She's here. Look who's here.' There was one moment of silence in which all their eyes turned to me – to weigh me up, I suppose. And I said, 'Good morning. My name is —' And there was this twanging sound like a bouncing spring – and they all just started falling about laughing. One of them had a steel ruler wedged under the edge of the table – I spotted it when he twanged it again. Renewed roars of laughter. And the laughter was out of all proportion to the joke. That's the thing. It was a feeble joke, even the first time. So why did they find it so bloody funny? And there was I, two paces into the room, red in the face and out of breath, desperately thinking: What do I do? What do I do?

Discussion

A good question. What *does* she do? We'll be coming back to that in some detail later. For the moment let's have a look at our questions, which focus on what has happened up to this point.

1. At what point, if any, during this scenario could Gloria have taken steps to improve her situation?

Most of us would probably be inclined to say that 'taking steps' was one of her mistakes. She'd have felt less flustered if she'd chosen to take the lift! But leaving that sort of advice aside, what could she have done? Was there an opportunity she missed?

I think there was. I think she could have used that encounter on the stairs to her advantage, and asked – even insisted – that the Section Head go up with her and introduce her to the class. If he was behaving professionally, instead of trying to wind her up, he would have offered to do this as a matter of courtesy, both to her and to the learners. This would have achieved several things. It would have given Gloria the opportunity to find out more practical information about the class as she and he walked up together; it would have allowed her to see how he interacted with the learners and whether there was anything in his approach that she could use; and it would have allowed her to enter the classroom initially as an observer for those first few crucial minutes while he was, nominally, in charge. Of course, he might have refused to do it, but it would certainly have been worth a try. One thing that Gloria's situation illustrates very clearly is the need for newly-appointed or inexperienced teachers to have the support of a mentor. For an inexperienced teacher to be confronted by a 'difficult' or challenging class without first being given the opportunity to see how a more experienced teacher manages them, is both unfair and unproductive. And indeed, the same principle applies for learner teachers engaged in teaching practice at a college. There is nothing to be gained, in terms of either learner or teacher learning, by setting them in front of badly behaved learners unless they've had the opportunity to see how an experienced teacher handles it. This provides them at least with a model of what does, or does not, work. It provides a starting point for reflection without crushing their confidence and enthusiasm. They – you, perhaps – have a right to ask for this kind of support. Gloria's Section Head, by the sound of it, couldn't care less about any of that. And that's a shame. But we've all met him, at some time, in some guise or another.

2. What, specifically, was she frightened of? What's the worst that could happen?

This is always a useful question – difficult to answer at the time, perhaps, but important to reflect upon after the panic has subsided. What Gloria fears here is what any of us would fear in such a situation: that's she's walking into a situation that she won't be able to control; that the learners are hostile and she will be the target of that hostility; that she won't be able to maintain her professional role – that her professional persona will disintegrate and she'll be reduced to the status of a victim who flees from the room or starts crying. For most of us, our self-esteem is partially dependent on our ability to carry out our professional role. Faith in this ability to carry out our role is very important to the way we feel about ourselves. Any threat to it is a very big deal. That's why Gloria, although she's not, as far as she knows, in any physical danger, is reacting with such a powerful fight or flight response. She feels threatened. She wants to run away. And it's made worse for her by the vague, unspecified dangers which the Section Head has gleefully hinted at:

> *I won't tell you what they did to the last bloke. Won't be seeing him again. I hope you last a bit longer. Doubt it, though.*

So there's this additional threat, although she has no idea of its exact nature. All she knows is that, if she's to conform to her own ideal of professional behaviour, she has to go in there and face it. Poor Gloria. We all know it's nerve-racking enough to face an unfamiliar group of learners for the first time, without being told vague horror stories about them first.

But what is the worst that can happen? If we're realistic, the worst that can happen is that her personal and professional confidence will receive a knock, and she will feel humiliated or be made to look silly in front of thirteen teenage boys. Bad enough, you might say. But then no one ever said that teaching was easy. The worst thing, in other words, is to encounter the class or the situation which brings you up against the limits of your own professional or personal ability to cope. Seen in this light, it may not be an entirely negative thing. We all do have limits. Part of being a professional is to be clear about where those limits are. We achieve this by reflecting on our experience and learning from it. We need to know our weaknesses as well as our strengths. Our weaknesses, or our areas for professional development, will change over time. But it's unlikely we'll ever all be excellent at everything. If we drive ourselves towards that goal we are letting ourselves in for a lot of stress and a sense of failure. In Chapter 2 we saw how some aspects of learner behaviour and motivation can be attributed to factors outside the teacher's control. We should always keep this in mind. In Gloria's case there is a possibility that a disastrous encounter with these learners might imply something other than a failure on her part. And even if it is a failure on her part, then at least she has learnt something about her current limitations and can plan her professional development accordingly.

3. **How would you interpret the learner behaviour that Gloria saw as she entered the room? What do you think this behaviour is communicating?**

4. **What are the possible reasons for the learners feeling like this?**

I'm going to take these two questions together, because it's likely that in considering your answers you've already linked the two. First of all it would be fair to guess that they're communicating a lack of interest in the subject they find themselves timetabled for – the subject Gloria's been brought in to teach them – Communication Skills. Given the Section Head's attitude, this is hardly surprising. He's already admitted he doesn't see the point of it; and this attitude may well have communicated itself to the learners. In any case, as far as they're concerned, they're in college to learn about Construction, and are probably of the view that anything else is a waste of time. We've also had a strong hint that their previous teacher found them too much to cope with. If this is so, the group has learnt that challenging behaviour works quite well at getting rid of the teacher and is therefore an effective way of avoiding having to do the subject. However, as we've learnt from Chapters 3 and 4, this sort of behaviour can be communicating other things, too. Perhaps some of them are intimidated by the subject, and are, under all the bravado, feeling as nervous as Gloria is that something is going to be demanded of them here that is beyond their capabilities; that they are going to be made to look foolish. Disruption may be their only way to stop this lesson happening. It's possible, too, that some of them may feel disturbed by what happened to the previous teacher. They may be uncomfortable with the idea that they were able to defeat the person who was supposed to be 'in charge'. This may have made them feel insecure or angry.

One thing is certain. This behaviour is not communicating any personal animus towards Gloria. How could it? They have never met her before. They don't know what sort of a person she is, nor what sort of a teacher she is. When they twang the ruler in order to make fun of her, and roar with laughter at her discomposure, it's not aimed at her specifically, but at the idea of 'Teacher'; or perhaps, in this case, the idea of 'Communication Teacher'. In other words they illustrate very nicely the tendency we discussed in Chapter 3 for learners to superimpose on any teacher the construct of Teacher-as-Villain which they have built out of their negative experiences. This is why she recognises, even in her panic, that the laughter is out of proportion to the joke. The learners' intent is to get at the Teacher. The joke is therefore just an excuse for them to laugh. It's an act of aggression, but it's not personal.

Would Gloria derive any comfort from understanding all this at the point at which it's happening? Perhaps. But it's hard to feel philosophical when you're also feeling frightened and being laughed at. So it would be expecting too much of anyone, I think, to feel perfectly comfortable in this situation. The crucial thing, however, will be how she answers her own question: 'What do I do?'

We left her standing just inside the classroom, holding her register and her folder of work, out of breath from the stairs, listening to a group of learners roaring with laughter at her expense. We're going to step now into the realms of science fiction and give Gloria two alternative futures with this class. The future she inhabits will depend on what she does next. This is the place at which the road forks. Let's say straight away, though, that if she takes the wrong fork this time and finds herself in the more difficult version of her future, there'll always be another fork – another chance to rescue the situation. That, after all, is what teaching and learning is like.

TASK TASK TASK **TASK** TASK TASK **TASK** TASK TASK **TASK** TASK TASK

So, here are the next pages of Gloria's journal in one of those two futures. Read them through carefully and consider what general guidelines we might draw from them about managing difficult behaviour and supporting learning.

'What do I do?' So I took a deep breath and grinned. A great big grin that crinkled up my eyes as though I really meant it. And I nodded at the lad with the steel ruler and made a mock bow. One of them shouted at him, 'She fancies you, Waheed!' And there was a bit of whistling. I walked to the table at the front, still grinning. I was trying to act as though I really wanted to be there. As though there was nowhere else I'd rather be. As though I'd been looking forward to this all week, and it was every bit as wonderful as I'd hoped it would be. This was pure survival. It seemed the only way to go. And I honestly think I'd have won an Oscar for it in a film. I put my stuff down and called to the lad on the windowsill, 'Thanks! Can you open the next one along as well? It's a bit stuffy in here.' Some more cat calls, but window boy seemed to like the attention. He opened the other top window and then jumped down and sat at his table (Thank goodness! Thank goodness!). I leaned against the table at the front and smiled round at them until I'd made eye contact with them all – except for Waheed, who was twanging away at his ruler. But it wasn't getting much of a laugh any more. It was probably getting on everybody else's nerves as much as it was on mine. And then one of them told him to 'Shut the **** up,' and then added, 'Whoops. Sorry, Miss.' Which got a bit of a laugh – but they were generally quietening down, the longer I stood there smiling, saying nothing. One of them shouted, 'What's she smiling at?' And then to me, 'What you smiling at?'

I said, 'I'll tell you in a minute. When you're all quiet.'

There was still a bit of sniggering and whispering to each other – looking at me out of the corner of their eyes – still trying to make me feel uncomfortable – and succeeding, though I wouldn't let them know it.

It was no good waiting for absolute quiet – I don't think that would've happened. So when it was about as quiet as I thought it would get, I said, 'I've been looking forward to meeting you lot. Mr P. [the Section Head]'s been telling me all about you.'

Groans. Shouts. 'What's he said, Miss?' 'Go on. What's he said?'

'Some good things. But one of the things he said was you didn't like Communication.'

Groans again. 'Waste of time', 'Rubbish' – and much worse. But there were quite a few of them wanting to know what good things he's said. I suppose that's human nature. And I think that was what I was banking on. But it was a bit tricky, because the horrible man hadn't said anything good about them at all. Anyway, I sort of struck a deal with them. I said that if they'd tell me, clearly and honestly, why they didn't like Communication, then I'd tell them all the good things Mr P. had said about them.

It got really interesting then. I actually forgot I was nervous of them, and started enjoying it. Some of them were even putting their hand up when they wanted to say something – wonderful how eleven years of schooling leaves its mark! I listed the main points they made on the flip chart. They included all the predictable things like:

Boring
Pointless
Takes up time they could be spending on other things
Won't ever be any use to them
And so on

I told them I was going to take it away and turn it into a sort of contract with them for next week – whereby if I could demonstrate to them that they were misjudging the subject, then they'd agree to revise their opinion of it. They jeered a bit at that – but it didn't matter because we were moving things forward and I still had most of their attention most of the time.

I said, 'OK. So do you want to hear some nice things about yourselves?' And I made out that Mr P. had said they were a very promising bunch, and that they were nice lads, and they had a good sense of humour.

Too bad if they ask him about this. It does no harm. And if he denies it – well – they'll just think he's pretending to be hard, but that really he praises them behind their backs. It was funny, though, because I could tell from their comments that they didn't really like him very much.

When I felt I'd really had enough of Waheed and his steel ruler, I said, 'Do you play any other instruments, Waheed?' They all laughed. And it was me who'd cracked the joke. That felt like a small victory of sorts.

Discussion

So is there anything we can generalise from this? Are there any guidelines, any rules of thumb we might draw from this version of Gloria's future? It goes without saying that we can't draw any hard and fast rules. What works in one situation with one particular group won't necessarily succeed in similar circumstances or with a different group. One of the things that makes dealing with this kind of behaviour challenging is that we often have to play it by ear. There is no foolproof set of procedures. Nevertheless, there is a number of general guidelines which we can bear in mind to help us; and Gloria's journal pages illustrate these for us.

✓ Gloria acts as though she's pleased to be there. She acts as though she was expecting to enjoy meeting the learners and enjoy the lesson with them. She gives no indication from her manner that she expects any trouble from them. Acting as though we are confident can, as cognitive psychologists will tell you, make us actually feel more confident. If we adopt the body language and expression of a confident person the feeling of confidence will often follow. One of the most obvious ways in which this works is that it affects how others respond to us. In this case, Gloria's learners are responding to an apparently confident teacher, one who seems pleased to be with them. This response of theirs, in turn, reinforces her confidence. In this way the relationship between the teacher and learners is moving in a positive direction. If, on the other hand, Gloria had let her fear and reluctance become apparent, the learners would probably have responded with a similar hostile negativity, which would exacerbate Gloria's lack of confidence.

✓ What Gloria succeeds in doing here is convincing the learners that she has positive expectations of them. She even, for good measure, makes up a story about their Section Head having positive expectations of them, too. If you look at how she deals with the learner on the windowsill, you see that she chooses to attribute a helpful motive to his being up there. He gets the message that she sees him not as a disruptive learner, but as a helpful one who is trying to open the window so that the classroom feels less stuffy. This is often worth a gamble. The learner must then choose which role to adopt – helpful or disruptive. But at least he has a choice. He has not been boxed into the role of disruptive learner from the start and therefore needn't feel compelled to play up to it. Similarly, Gloria puts the best possible construction on the classroom banter. When the learners shout, 'What's she smiling at?' and 'What you smiling at?' she chooses not to interpret this as rude or aggressive, but as a genuine question which she promises to answer. She is signalling to the learners that she expects to like them, and that they are living up to her expectations.

✓ She is also able to use humour to help defuse aggression and to indicate that they are all – learners and teacher – on the same side. When she asks Waheed whether he plays any other instruments, she's not only telling him in a non-aggressive way that they're all a bit bored now with the noise he's making; she's also subtly altering the dynamics in that room. For a moment it is no longer learners v. teacher, but everyone irritated by the noise Waheed is making v. Waheed. The learners laugh at her joke, rather than at the twang of the ruler. In this way she brings peer pressure to bear rather than using direct confrontation. She is able to signal her expectation of an orderly working environment and a friendly working atmosphere without having to get angry or unfriendly. Did you notice, also, that she capitalised on the noisy reception they gave her by taking the opportunity to memorise Waheed's name? She was then able to play this card later for maximum impact.

✓ Gloria starts by finding out what the learners' expectations are. She asks for their views about the subject, and validates their responses by showing that she takes them seriously. In this way, she signals that they are in this together; that there is room for negotiation; that this is not a learner v. teacher situation, but a team effort to which both teacher and learners can contribute.

✓ Taken together, the various aspects of Gloria's behaviour make it very difficult for the learners to continue superimposing the Teacher-as-Villain construct on her. In other words, she challenges their own expectations and – with luck – encourages them to rethink.

To summarise then: the strategies that Gloria is using here are:

- **acting confidently and appearing pleased to be teaching the class;**
- **making the learners feel that she and others have good expectations of them;**
- **putting the best possible interpretation on learners' behaviour and playing things down;**
- **using humour to defuse hostility;**
- **discussing the learners' own views and expectations;**
- **challenging the Teacher-as-Enemy stereotype;**
- **quickly learning some names.**

We must beware, of course, of taking a sentimental Hollywood approach to this. The 'Dynamic Teacher Wins Over Troublesome Class' scenario is rarely as simple as that in real life. Gloria's strategy, in this version of events, has proved successful in this particular class on this particular day. This is not to say that the strategy would be foolproof for every group of learners, nor that this class will be easy to face next time she meets them. What we can take from this account are ideas and guidelines that may help us when we find ourselves facing similarly challenging situations. The extent to which these strategies work in any instance will depend on many factors; but whether they succeed or fail, they provide a useful starting point for reflection.

CLOSE FOCUS CLOSE FOCUS CLOSE FOCUS **CLOSE FOCUS** CLOSE FOCUS CLOSE FOCUS

Some of Gloria's strategies were high risk. You might like to discuss, in your journal or with your mentor:

- **the Health and Safety implications of the way Gloria dealt with the learner on the windowsill;**

- **the ethical implications of pretending to the learners that the Section Head had spoken well of them;**

- **the acceptability of a joke made at one learner's expense.**

We've seen one version of Gloria's future. Let's put her back in the doorway now and look at an alternative version of what might have happened.

TASK TASK TASK **TASK** TASK TASK **TASK** TASK TASK **TASK** TASK TASK

Read Gloria's account of this alternative version of the same lesson, and consider the following questions.

1. At what point did things begin going wrong?

2. Can you identify any occasions on which there was an opportunity to 'rescue' the situation?

'What do I do?' So I took a deep breath and said, 'Alright now. Settle down. And you,' to the boy with the steel ruler, 'put that away. And you,' to the boy on the windowsill, 'get down from there before you fall. Get down, now.'

He waved his arms about and did a good impression of someone losing their balance. Then he flapped his arms as though he was going to fly. The others were all hooting and shouting. I slammed my folder and the register down on the nearest table and shouted, 'I said get down. Now.' He jumped down and half landed on one of the other boys and they started a bit of a scuffle. The steel ruler twanged again, like a sound effect, and the ones who weren't watching the 'fight' laughed with delight. So I said, 'Give me that!' He meekly held out the ruler towards me and then as I went to grasp it, he snatched it away, slipped it under the table top and twanged it again. I said, 'Yes. Very funny. I suppose you've heard the saying, Small things amuse small minds.'

They leapt on this, of course. Lots of innuendo about 'small things'. Lots of laughing and pointing. I should have seen it coming, I suppose. But I was distracted by this scuffle going on. It wasn't a fight really, because it wasn't serious. But it was distracting everyone's attention and obviously I couldn't let it go. So I said, 'Come on. Settle down. Stop that. It's like being with a bunch of animals.' Then, of course, the animal noises started. I was thinking, 'Oh no. If anyone hears this going on they're going to think I'm a complete loser. They'll never give me a full-time job.' And I found myself really hating these students for putting me through this. What had I ever done to them?

When that boy twanged the ruler again it was the last straw. I said, 'Here! Give that to me! Now!'

He put it behind his back, grinning.

I said, 'Now! Or else!'

The boy behind him said, 'Or else what?' And someone else made that silly surprised exclamation: 'Ooooo!'

So I said, 'Or else you can get out!'

Then lots of them joined in with this 'Oooooo!' noise. I shouted at them, 'Just settle down!' The scuffle was still going on, and I couldn't tell now whether it was still in fun. Then I glanced in the other direction and saw that a couple of them had picked up my file and the register. They were writing in the register – they seemed to be making alterations in it and laughing and showing it to the table behind them. I said, 'Give it to me.' And then someone shouted, 'Go on. She wants you to give it to her.' Roars of laughter. I couldn't let this go. So I told the boy who'd shouted to get out. He didn't budge. And then I just lost it. I shouted at the top of my voice, 'Get out!' But they all just laughed. I made a grab for the register and it tore in half. They thought this was hilarious. 'Look what you done now, Miss!'

'Well that's about what you deserve. Half a register – for a bunch of half-wits. If you think I'm going to waste my time with you, you've got another think coming.' And I walked out. I still can't believe I did it. I just walked out. With my half of the register. I'd never even got as far as the teacher's table. Why should I put up with that sort of thing? Whatever they paid me, it still wouldn't be worth it.

Discussion

And so Gloria walks out. The trouble is, this makes it very difficult to walk back in again, and most teachers' contracts will require them to do just that. This version of events is not a comfortable one to read, but there's a great deal to be learned from it. Let's take our first question.

1. At what point did things begin going wrong?

I don't think they were destined to go wrong from the start. Gloria's firm approach – her initial efforts to establish order by asking the learner to get down from the windowsill and the other to stop playing with the ruler – was a perfectly reasonable one. Many of us would have started off that way. She was laying her ground rules for acceptable behaviour and acting appropriately in her role as classroom manager. I think the point at which it began to go wrong was when she responded to the boy on the windowsill like this:

> *I slammed my folder and the register down on the nearest table and shouted, 'I said get down. Now.'*

This display of anger was, I think, a mistake. Showing that you are angry can send the wrong signals. Someone who feels completely in control of a situation doesn't usually need to flare up with anger. Gloria therefore weakens her position by getting angry at this point – within only a few minutes of meeting the group. She also escalates the confrontation. There was still room at this point to respond to his bird imitations with a long-suffering smile, a few nods, and a quiet, 'Come on.'

2. Can you identify any occasions on which there was an opportunity to 'rescue' the situation?

The reality is that every minute Gloria spends in that classroom presents an opportunity to rescue the situation. Until she storms out. Then it becomes very difficult to rescue indeed.

As the seconds ticked by, however, she only succeeded in making the situation worse and worse. Here are some of the mistakes and misjudgements you are likely to have identified.

✗ She makes it clear to the learners that she doesn't like being with them.

✗ She makes it clear that she has low expectations of them.

✗ She turns every incident into a confrontation.

✗ She causes every confrontation to escalate, instead of playing it down or defusing it.

✗ She interprets all learner behaviour as hostile.

✗ She makes a big deal out of every small incident (instead of addressing the potentially serious issue of a scuffle that may be turning into a fight).

✗ She doesn't choose her words carefully, with the result that she fuels the learners' enjoyment of innuendo.

✗ She displays no sense of humour, nor any other trait that would dispose the learners to like her.

Of these two alternative scenarios, I would prefer to think that Gloria stepped into the first. But even if she stepped into the second, there would be a great deal she could learn from the experience if she took the time to analyse and reflect.

We began this chapter with a metaphor about battles. We could interpret Gloria's two alternative realities as a battle won and a battle lost. The first a victory, the second a defeat. But the battle isn't between the teacher and the learners. If the learners don't learn and don't find their learning worthwhile, then everyone loses. The battle – if we're going to call it that – is for the hearts and minds of the learners. It is one that is fought to motivate them and to develop their potential. And one of the ways we can win it is to let them know that we have great expectations of them; not necessarily in the sense of high achievement, but rather an expectation that we can enjoy working together towards whatever goals are appropriate to them.

A SUMMARY OF KEY POINTS A SUMMARY OF KEY POINTS A SUMMARY OF KEY POINTS

In this chapter we have:

> explored the idea that positive expectations of learners may have a positive impact on their achievement and behaviour;

> considered the importance of viewing learning not as some sort of battle between teacher and learners, but as a goal shared by both;

> emphasised the importance of regarding learner behaviour as a means by which they are communicating something – and perhaps something it is useful to know – to the teacher.

Branching options

The following three options are designed to provide you with additional opportunities for reflection, analysis and research. You may choose the option which best supports your currently identified needs, as set out, for example, in your action plan for a teaching qualification or for your continuing professional development (CPD). Alternatively, you may choose to work through two or even all three tasks.

1. *Reflection*
   - Think back to the last occasion in your teaching where at some point learner behaviour presented a barrier to learning. Did you expect this behaviour from this particular learner? How did you interpret that behaviour at the time? On reflection, might there be some alternative way of reading what was happening? Was your specialist subject relevant here?
   - How did you manage the incident? Did your response to the learner signal that you were surprised they would behave in this way; or did it suggest that you expected no better?
   - Is there anything you would change about your response if this situation arose again?

2. *Analysis*
   - Choosing a class which presents you with behaviour management issues, take particular notice of the patterns of behaviour next time you teach them. For example, what 'sets them off'; who takes the lead; who is cooperative and how do they respond to those who aren't; does your specialist subject provide excuses or opportunities for this sort of behaviour? If possible, note down any observations which surprise you or which you feel may be important factors in the group's behaviour.
   - The next couple of times you teach this group, experiment with *great expectations*: try reflecting back to the learners a positive reinterpretation of their behaviour; take (or even make) every opportunity to praise them; tell them how much you enjoy teaching them.
   - See whether you notice any change in their behaviour and levels of cooperation. Use your original notes as the point of comparison.
   - Look out for any changes in their attitude towards their own learning. For example, do they become more inclined to take ownership of it?

3. *Research*
   - Use the internet or your library access to explore what other writers have to say about the link between expectations of learners and their performance. If possible, find out what has been said in relation to your own subject.
   - It's likely that you'll find there's some disagreement over this, as over most theories. Which (or whose) arguments do you find most convincing, and why?
   - How will you apply what you've learnt to your own professional practice?

REFERENCES AND FURTHER READING REFERENCES AND FURTHER READING

Ball, S., Maguire, M. and Macrae, S. (2000) *Choice, Pathways and Transitions Post-16: New Youth, New Economies in the Global City*. London: Routledge.

Martinez, P. (2000) *Raising Achievement: A Guide to Successful Strategies*. London: FEDA.

Wallace, S. (2011) *Teaching, Tutoring and Training in the Lifelong Learning Sector*, 4th edition. Exeter: Learning Matters.

7
Breaking out

*Discovery consists of seeing what everybody has
seen and thinking what nobody has thought.*
Albert von Szent-Gyorgyi, 1962

The objectives of this chapter

This chapter is about thinking 'outside the box'. First it examines a range of currently accepted
theories of learning, and tries them out on familiar classroom situations. In this way it illustrates
and discusses their usefulness and their limitations in helping us to better understand how learners may be motivated and positive behaviour encouraged. It then goes on to demonstrate how
teachers themselves can theorise from their own experience, and how such theorising may help
them to develop the strategies which work most effectively for their learners.

Introduction: theories of learning

If we turn to the textbooks on learning theory to try to understand why our learners are
confrontational or appear disinclined to engage with their learning, we will find no short-
age of theoretical answers and advice. Often this can help us to understand why a
learner or learners are behaving in a certain way, but it doesn't always help us to understand what we can do about it in terms of specific, realistic, day-to-day strategies. In the
first part of this chapter, we're going to have a look at three learning theorists whose
work has informed much recent and current thinking in education. Broadly speaking,
they approach an individual's readiness or willingness to learn as a psychological issue.
In Chapter 2 we saw that there may be other factors – historical, practical, sociological
and economic – which underlie some of the difficult situations which teachers in the FE
sector are faced with in the classroom and the workshop. In the process of considering
what the learning theorists have to say, we should keep this wider context in mind and
we shall be exploring it in more detail in Chapter 12. Real life is rarely as clear cut as text-
book answers might suggest. No theory, however inspired, will work for every situation,
every time. When we confront a difficult situation with our learners – whether it be lack
of motivation or inappropriate behaviour – the causes are likely to be complex. That is
why finding the answer is not always easy.

According to Maslow (1954 and 1987), part of the answer may be found by taking into
consideration what he would term our learners' 'hierarchy of needs'. As human beings,
our more basic needs, such as the need for comfort or for safety, must be met before we
can turn our attention to satisfying our higher-order needs. Achieving our potential
through learning is one of these higher-order needs. Therefore, Maslow would argue, if a
learner is cold, or uncomfortable, or frightened or has certain worries on their mind, they
won't be able to turn their attention to learning, until these lower-order needs are met.
This hierarchy of needs is usually represented as a pyramid, with basic physiological
needs forming the broad base, and with self-actualisation at the apex. In a simplified version, it would look something like this.

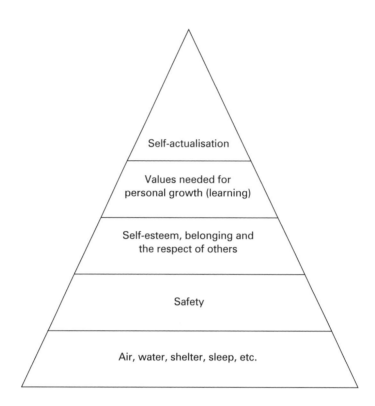

On a very basic level, then, this would mean that in a chilly classroom our best first step towards getting the learners to attend to their learning will be to turn on the radiators. Any other strategy we use – such as encouragement, or devising fascinating activities for them to do – will have only limited success until their basic need for a tolerable temperature to work in is met.

Now, let's consider this for a moment in the light of what we have read in Chapter 2. If Maslow is right and a sense of self-worth or the feeling that we are valued by others is also a prerequisite for our receptivity to learning, then we can see why learners who fared badly in school, who associate education with personal failure or who feel they are being 'fobbed off' with a training that will never lead to real employment, would appear unwilling or unready to learn. Similarly, we can see why, if learners are afraid that their inability or ignorance will be exposed, or if they're afraid of mockery from their peers or admonishment from their teacher, that fear – the feeling that they are not safe – will operate to block their co-operation and engagement with their learning. What is immediately apparent here is that there is only so much that the teacher can do to remedy this. Maslow's theory is helpful in explaining why some learners are disinclined to learn; but if their fear or lack of self-esteem owes some of its origins to factors which are sociological, economic or historical, then the teacher has only a limited scope for applying Maslow's theory to remedying the lack of motivation or inability to learn. In other words, it may have wider application as a diagnostic tool than as a remedial one. We shall come back to this point later in the chapter when we apply the theory to a real-life situation.

Let's have a look now at another commonly cited theory of learning: the Neo-behaviourist model. The famous name here is Skinner (1938). At its most simple level, this theory has been taken to mean that we are motivated by reward or the avoidance of pain, and that the consequences of our actions or responses may lead us to change those actions or responses. For example, if I'm praised for attempting to answer a question, even if I get it wrong, I'll be more inclined to risk offering an answer the next time, too. If, on the other hand, the teacher just snaps 'No!' and goes on to ask someone else, I'll be less likely to risk the loss of face next time. Praise from the teacher is known, in Neo-behaviourist terms, as positive reinforcement. Positive reinforcement makes the recipient feel good, so they're more likely to repeat that behaviour so as to get that good feeling – that reward – again. This same dynamic can work in a less obvious and less positive way, too. If a learner is being disruptive and, as a consequence, getting lots of attention from the teacher (even though the attention may be of the negative, 'Sit down and shut up' kind), that very attention may be seen as a pay-off and may therefore reinforce the disruptive behaviour. The thinking here is: 'Having the teacher shout at me is better than getting no attention at all.'

Learners who are moving towards the apex of Maslow's hierarchy, and are beginning to find that learning is a pleasure and a fulfilment in itself, will be moving towards becoming life-long learners, because, the Neo-behaviourists would say, learning is now providing its own reinforcement. But again, if we look at this theory of rewards and reinforcement in the light of Chapter 2, we see that the task facing us is not always going to be easily solved at the level of the individual teacher in the individual classroom. The learner coming into FE is likely to have already had at least eleven years' experience of education during which certain behaviours have been reinforced. If he or she has already learnt that one consequence of disruptive behaviour is that it helps avoid pain – that is, it avoids having to get down to work which may be painfully difficult or may painfully expose their lack of ability – then you, the teacher, will have years of reinforcement to undo. But you will have to undo it if you are to support that individual's learning. And one way you can do that is by reinforcing positive behaviour and by removing the pay-off for negative behaviour. Removing the pay-off for negative behaviour is more easily said than done. In effect it means that you don't allow the learner's disruptive behaviour to provide a way for them to avoid engaging with their learning. And that's a tall order. We'll see later in the chapter how it might work.

The third learning theory we're going to consider here is that of Rogers (1983), who is usually spoken of as belonging to the Humanist school of learning theorists. According to the Humanists, the key factor in motivating learning is the quality of the relationship between the learner and the teacher. Each learner must be respected and valued for who and what she is; and a relationship of trust must be built between the teacher and the learner. This is expressed by Rogers in the phrase 'unconditional positive regard'. The teacher should demonstrate unconditional positive regard for each learner, and in this way build a relationship in which learning can take place.

We can see at once how this theory relates on the one hand to Maslow's proposition and, on the other, to ideas of the behaviourists. Genuine trust and respect from the teacher would dispose the learner to feel safe and valued, and would be likely to raise her self-esteem. In terms of Maslow's hierarchy this would provide the conditions in which learning would be more likely to take place. And if the teacher is rewarding the learner with trust and with respect just for being in a learning situation, then the Neo-behaviourists would agree that this would work very well as positive reinforcement. But what about a situation in which a learner is behaving badly or disruptively? Wouldn't the 'positive regard' of the teacher in this context simply reinforce the undesirable behaviour? This is a good example to bear in mind in order to remind ourselves that the various learning theories do not always converge, and may even conflict. It is part of our function as professionals to weigh such theories against our own experience, and to decide what is useful to take from them and what is not.

Can you identify any other ways in which the learning theories we have looked at might be considered to contradict one another? Take some time to think how each might apply to a specific incident from your own professional practice.

We are now going to look at a 'real-life' incident faced by a newly-appointed teacher, and we are going to consider how he might formulate his response to this according to each of the learning theories outlined above. We are then going to ask ourselves whether there might be any other options open to him, or any advice we might want to give him. In other words, we are going to weigh the theory against a rather more pragmatic approach in order to identify strategies that could be of practical use to us.

Patrick

The journal entries below describe one teacher's experience of a learner's challenging behaviour. This is a situation which builds up over time, and the learner is one with whom the teacher has regular contact.

When you have read this teacher's account, make some notes on how he might handle the situation if he were to base his strategy on what he knows about learning theory according to:

(a) **Maslow;**

(b) **The Neo-behaviourists;**

(c) **Rogers.**

You'll find a discussion of his possible responses after the journal extracts.

Friday

Not a very good week. I was looking forward to working with the Return to Learning group, partly because they're all adults – most of them in their thirties – and partly because I think this is what FE should be all about. The sector of the second chance – all that stuff. People who've dropped out of education because it's part of their pattern of social deprivation. These are the people I want to help. This is what I'm in it for. But there's a woman in this group and I just know she's going to be trouble. She whines. I know that's not a very professional remark to make – but it's true. You'd think nobody else in the group has any problems, and you'd think all her problems were my fault. The teachers who made her feel bad at school; the people who design forms she can't understand. All my fault. At least, you'd think so. Anyway, today we were doing a session on letter writing, and she's not doing anything, not even picking up her pen, not even trying. So I say to her something like, 'Come on, Charmaine. This is useful stuff. You never know when you'll need it.' But she does this big laugh and says in her loud voice, 'No way! What do I want to write letters for when I've got a phone?' And she looks round at the others for support, and they just look back a bit warily. I think they're a bit scared of her (I know I am!). And I try to explain how a letter is sometimes more appropriate than the phone, but I'm thinking to myself that really I should be going around the room helping the others instead of giving so much time to her. But as soon as I move off to help someone else, she starts making a call on her mobile! Can you believe it?! So I go back to her and ask her to put it away and I remind her of our ground-rules. And the conversation goes like this:

'It's urgent.'

'Well, what's it about?'

'I'm not telling you.'

'Well, if you've got to make a call, why don't you go outside and make it?'

'You chucking me out?'

'No. I'm just saying —'

'That's effing charming, that is. I've got a sick kiddy at home and you want to chuck me out for —'

'I don't want to chuck you out —'

'Good. Right then.'

And she carries on making her call. Incredible! And there's no way that call was to a child. She was arranging to go out after college, and cackling like a demented chicken. And I'm sorry. I know that's unprofessional. But she makes me so angry, and there's nothing I can do about it. Never mind. At least it's the weekend.

Tuesday
The charming Charmaine again. How aptly named. Turns out she's been to see the Head of Department and told him I'm victimising her for being a single mother. Me! So Derek had me in for this chat, and there I was, having to defend myself. I think he believed me. He must have done, mustn't he? The irony is, she's the very type of student I came into this game to help. And I feel guilty enough anyway because I find her so irritating. And the knowledge that she wants to cause trouble for me makes me even less inclined to like her. And there she was in the class again this afternoon, watching me. And so I was exaggeratedly nice to her – smiled at her, asked her view on every topic (to which she replied indignantly every time, 'I dunno.'), and generally gritted my teeth and tried to be professional. About half way through the lesson, lo and behold! She gets her phone out and starts making a call. I look at her and she holds my gaze with this triumphant look, like she was saying, 'Go on, just try it. You daren't, dare you? Because I've got you now, and you know it.'

I just let it go. If she wants to play games, she can play them on her own.

Friday
Well, I think I've just about reached rock bottom, now. The lovely Charmaine has been to see Derek again, and told him that I'm ignoring her. I'm helping everyone else, apparently, but not giving her any help at all. Correct. Spot on. Because she's not doing any work. So what am I supposed to help her with? Am I supposed to spend half the lesson pleading with her to do some work, just to help her fill in the time between phone calls? I said to Derek, I'm there to help the students who want to learn (never thought I'd hear myself saying something like that). And he said, no. He said we've a responsibility to support the learning of *all* our students. So there we are. I can now consider myself well and truly told off. Thanks, Charmaine.

The question is, what can I do? I've got to turn this around somehow.

Discussion

If Patrick turned to our theorists for some ideas, these are the sort of analyses and strategies he might come up with.

MASLOW

Basing his analysis on Maslow, he might decide that what was probably hampering Charmaine's motivation to learn was a very low sense of self-esteem or a sense of insecurity about being in the classroom situation, or probably both; the one leading to the other. If she feels unsafe in the classroom and lacks confidence in her own abilities, these factors will act as barriers to her learning. Until she feels relatively safe and confident she will resist any encouragement to learn. According to this interpretation, her phone calls and her complaints are either avoidance devices or efforts to raise her own self-esteem by making herself feel empowered, or both of these. So, how can Patrick use this theory to inform his practice? Well, he could try to reassure Charmaine that she is welcome. He could try to make her feel valued. He could praise any efforts she makes in order to raise her sense of self-worth. But in practical terms what does this really mean? He seems to have tried the first two, but got little response

> *And so I was exaggeratedly nice to her – smiled at her, asked her view on every topic (to which she replied indignantly every time, 'I dunno.')*

And how is he to try the third if she makes no effort and produces no work for him to praise? The theory, therefore, may be quite useful in helping Patrick to understand why Charmaine is behaving as she is, and it will provide general pointers towards how to put things right; but in this case there's no obvious practical solution to be found here.

NEO-BEHAVIOURISTS

Basing his analysis on the Neo-behaviourists, Patrick might find himself even more disheartened. Charmaine's uncooperative and confrontational behaviour has already yielded her several rewards. Her aggressive attitude has, as far she's concerned, won her the right to make phone calls in class. Her complaints to the HoD have been rewarded by putting her in a position where the teacher is nervous of challenging her if she refuses to work or to abide by the rules. In other words, her bad behaviour has really paid off for her. She has learnt that it works. She's learnt that it gets her what she wants. Now, the sensible strategy for Patrick, obviously, is to apply Neo-behaviourist theory to encourage her to learn that such behaviour *doesn't* pay, and that learning and cooperation can be even more rewarding than argument and non-cooperation. Everyone, I'm sure, would agree that this makes absolute sense. But how does he go about this in practical terms, given the situation he finds himself in? He could praise every sign of cooperation; but so far there appears to have been none. He could withhold reward when her behaviour falls outside acceptable parameters – or could he? Already she has complained about him denying her his attention:

> *The lovely Charmaine has been to see Derek again, and told him that I'm ignoring her. I'm helping everyone else, apparently, but not giving her any help at all.*

Again, the theory proves useful as a diagnostic tool, but doesn't necessarily provide the necessary guidance on a practical level as to what Patrick can do next.

ROGERS

Basing his analysis on Rogers' Humanist approach, Patrick might come to the conclusion that what is holding Charmaine back is a lack of trust in the teacher–learner relationship. She doesn't feel unconditionally valued and accepted, and therefore is not motivated to learn. So, what's Patrick going to do about that? Here we come up against one of the problems with Rogers' 'unconditional positive regard'. It's not always possible to feel this for a learner. In fact, it's quite clear from his journal that Patrick has come to actively dislike this particular learner, and he is worried that this is somehow unprofessional of him. It would be unprofessional, I believe, if he were to make this dislike apparent. He is only human after all, and cannot control what he feels. But if he is sufficiently self-aware to be clear about what he is feeling – and his reflective journal will help him here – then he can make sure that this does not in any way affect the way he behaves towards this particular learner. In other words, we may not always feel unconditional positive regard for our learners, but we can behave towards them as though we do. And this can work, in terms of motivation. Think of Gloria in Chapter 6. When she acted as though she was enjoying teaching that particular class, the learners began to respond to her more positively.

'Ah,' you might say, 'but wait a moment. I've read the earlier part of this chapter. If Patrick behaves towards Charmaine as though his positive regard for her is *unconditional*, how does that square with the Neo-behaviourist notion that he should only reward or reinforce her behaviour when it is acceptable or appropriate?' The answer is that it doesn't, really; and so Patrick, and you, and I, will always have to make a choice.

TASK TASK TASK **TASK** TASK TASK **TASK** TASK TASK **TASK** TASK TASK

What would you advise Patrick to do? What strategy or strategies do you think might work, and why? You might like to jot down some notes on this, or record your reflections in your journal, before reading on.

So, where does all this leave Patrick? He probably has a better idea now of why Charmaine is behaving in the way she is; but he may be no further forward in developing a strategy for motivating her or managing her behaviour.

Discussion

Patrick could use what he has learnt about the probable causes of Charmaine's behaviour in the following way. He could speak to her after the lesson. In view of the fact that she has already been telling lies about him, he would be wise to do this in a public space, and preferably with a witness. Another colleague or another learner, or both, would be better than Derek the HoD, because having the latter there might lead Charmaine to believe that Patrick was only speaking to her under duress. If, however, she declines to speak with him, he will probably have to ask for a three-way meeting with Derek present.

Let's assume, though, that she agrees. This, then, is Patrick's opportunity to express concern that they have got off on the wrong foot; to tell her how much he admires her for returning to education; how he came into teaching just for the opportunity to teach learners like her; that he would like to discover how she feels about the class and how he can best tailor it to meet her needs. From what we have read in his journal, we know all this to be perfectly true. And by saying it to Charmaine, and making sure she hears it, he is putting into practice some of the key points from the learning theory we've discussed. He is showing Charmaine that he values her as a learner and wants to establish a more positive and caring basis for their professional relationship; and he is emphasising the human to human – rather than teacher to learner – nature of their interaction (Rogers). In this way he is, hopefully, making her feel more secure and raising her self-esteem (Maslow); and he is rewarding her co-operation (agreeing to talk with him) by giving her lots of validation – letting her hear positive things said about her (Neo-behaviourist).

I think this is probably his best shot. It may not work immediately. He may have to do it more than once. In fact, he may have to do it several times. And each time he will have to swallow his irritation and his indignation, and make Charmaine feel that he means what he is saying. This is part of being a professional – the ability not to take things personally, or at least to behave as though you don't. Of course, it may never work, and at some point he will have to weigh up the needs of Charmaine against those of the other learners and take the matter back to Derek the HoD and thrash things out. But first he has to try, because by not giving up straightaway there's a possibility he may make a real difference to this learner's future.

CLOSE FOCUS CLOSE FOCUS CLOSE FOCUS CLOSE FOCUS CLOSE FOCUS **CLOSE FOCUS**

If you disagree with this strategy, or if your suggested strategy is very different, take the opportunity to discuss this with a colleague or a mentor. Remember, there are no right answers. A strategy is only a solution if it works; and what works in one instance is not guaranteed to work in another.

Identifying your own theories of motivation and learning

One of the advantages of keeping a reflective journal is that you are able to identify, examine and test your own accumulation of propositional knowledge – the professional wisdom that you gain from your experience. This is what reflective practice and continuing professional development are about. You may, for example, already have encountered a learner like Charmaine and discovered for yourself a means of motivating and engaging her. Whatever general principle you brought to bear in that instance, will, if it was successful, be the one you are most likely to apply if you encounter such a situation again. In this way you have come up with your own practice-based theory; and each time you apply it, you will be testing it and refining it, until you have a pretty good idea of when it will work and when it won't. But this testing and reflection is a continuous process. It isn't something that just finishes – for example when you get your teaching qualification or when you've been teaching for five years. It is part of the ongoing function of a professional to be theorising and testing that theory.

One way to begin to identify your personal theories about what motivates learners and how they learn is to read factual or fictional accounts of teaching and learning and, first of all, to identify the theories which seem to underlie the practice, and then to judge the extent to which these coincide or conflict with your own. Even if you can only identify what you disagree with, this is a good place to start.

TASK TASK TASK **TASK** TASK TASK **TASK** TASK TASK **TASK** TASK TASK

Read the two passages below and decide

(a) **what each implies about the teacher's theory of how to motivate learners;**

(b) **what each implies about the teacher's theory of what education is for;**

(c) **the extent to which you agree or disagree with each.**

Passage 1

As I keep saying, let all the lessons of young people take the form of doing rather than talking; don't set them to learn things from books that they can learn from experience. It's ridiculous to try to give them practice in persuasive speaking when they have nothing to say, or to expect to make them feel in the classroom the power of passionate speaking or all the forcefulness of a good argument when they have nothing and nobody to persuade! All the rules of rhetoric are just a waste of words to those who do not know how to use them for their own purposes. What does it matter to a learner to know how Hannibal encouraged his soldiers to cross the Alps? If instead of those great speeches you showed him how to talk his prefect into giving him a holiday, you can be certain he would pay more attention to your rules.

Jean-Jacques Rousseau: *Emile* (1772)

Passage 2

'This is the first class in English spelling and philosophy ... Now, then, where's the first boy?'

'Please, sir, he's cleaning the back parlour window,' said the temporary head of the philosophical class.

'So he is, to be sure,' rejoined Squeers. 'We go upon the practical mode of teaching, Nickleby; the regular education system. C-l-e-a-n, clean, verb active, to make bright, to scour. W-i-n, win, d-e-r, der, winder, a casement. When the boy knows this out of the book, he goes and does it. It's just the same principle as the use of the globes. Where's the second boy?'

'Please, sir, he's weeding the garden,' replied a small voice.

'To be sure,' said Squeers, by no means disconcerted. 'So he is. B-o-t, bot, t-i-n, tin, n-e-y, ney, bottiney, noun substantive, a knowledge of plants. When he has learnt that bottiney means a knowledge of plants, he goes and knows 'em. That's our system, Nickleby; what do you think of it?'

'It's a very useful one, at any rate,' answered Nicholas ...

'Let any boy speak a word without leave,' said Mr Squeers mildly, 'and I'll take the skin off his back.'

This special proclamation had the desired effect, and a death-like silence immediately prevailed.

Charles Dickens: *Nicholas Nickleby* (1839)

Discussion

Passage 1

(a) What is implied about the teacher's theory of motivation? This was written a long time ago, but what the writer is suggesting here is something that still forms part of most debates about education today. He is arguing that the learner needs to see that what they are learning is useful *for their own purposes*. There's an important distinction to be made here between this and the idea of seeing their learning as being useful to society in general or to the economic well-being of that society. The theory of motivation that's being expounded here is that young people will be better motivated if they recognise that what they are learning is relevant to their immediate situation, and if they are encouraged to learn it by trying it out rather than just hearing about it.

(b) So what does this imply about what the writer thinks education is for? It would seem to follow from what we have just said that this writer believes education to be about the development of the individual, rather than, say, about serving some collective purpose such as building a better-educated workforce. We could perhaps make a link here to the liberal model of education: the idea that education should not be about fitting us for work, but about enabling each of us to fulfil our individual potential.

CLOSE FOCUS CLOSE FOCUS CLOSE FOCUS CLOSE FOCUS CLOSE FOCUS **CLOSE FOCUS**

Take a moment here to consider your own views about this. On an imaginary continuum, with education as a means of meeting the needs of the individual at one end and education as a means of meeting the needs of society and the economy at the other, what position best represents your point of view?

Education should serve the needs of...

The individual ←⎯⎯⎯⎯⎯⎯⎯→ Society

Or would you want to argue, perhaps, that the need for fulfilling one's potential, and those collective socio-economic needs as defined by governments, will always coincide?

Passage 2

(a) What is implied about the teacher's theory of motivation?

Well, I think we could safely say that Mr Squeers subscribes to the Neo-behaviourist school, although he applies the theory in a rather negative way.

> *'Let any boy speak a word without leave,' said Mr Squeers mildly, 'and I'll take the skin off his back.'*

He motivates by threat of punishment. The reward for obedience is to withhold the punishment. Remember, a central tenet of Neo-behaviourist thought is that we learn from the consequences of our actions. If, as a consequence of talking, we lose the skin from our backs, we'll pretty quickly learn to keep quiet.

(b) What's Mr Squeers' theory about what education is for? Well, Nicholas sums this up nicely:

> *'It's a very useful one, at any rate,' answered Nicholas.*

There's a joke here, but 170 years on, most of us will miss it. In Dickens's day the education of gentlemen was in grammar and the classical languages; but for the less elevated classes it was considered that an education should be 'useful'. There was much discussion of what constituted 'Useful Knowledge', and a great deal of mockery by progressive educators who came up with the scornful term 'Really Useful Knowledge'. All this forms part of the origins of our current and ongoing debate about academic v. vocational qualifications. Mr Squeers, however, takes 'usefulness' to new heights (or depths). His theory about learning seems to boil down to simply this: education is purely instrumental – a means to an end. The 'theory' – how to spell (or rather, how to mis-spell) 'window' is simply a device to lend respectability to what is, in effect, an undemanding, learning-by-doing, skills course, which – and this is presumably its most useful aspect – also gets Mr Squeers' windows cleaned and his garden weeded. Anyone feeling a little cynical about recent policies relating to training schemes or vocational routes through school might be tempted to read this passage as a metaphor for all that is undesirable about employer-led or workforce-oriented 'education'. Mr Squeers seems to believe that the 'usefulness' of what is learnt will itself justify the learning. But his theory leaves a major question unanswered, for who is to define what is and what is not 'useful' and what does and does not constitute 'education'? What seems certain is that Mr Squeers' definition does not involve learning being useful to the individual nor to any wider social purpose.

(c) How far do you agree or disagree with the theories implicit in this passage?

Hopefully, on reflection, you will find that your own views and theories do not entirely converge with Squeers'. If they do – well, that's one way of getting your windows clean.

A SUMMARY OF KEY POINTS A SUMMARY OF KEY POINTS A SUMMARY OF KEY POINTS

In this chapter we have:

> considered how we might apply Maslow's theory of the *Hierarchy of Needs* in order to understand and address issues about learners' behaviour;

> explored ways in which we can apply Neo-behaviourist theory in order to understand and address learners' behaviour;

> discussed how we can apply Rogerian Humanist theory in order to understand and address learners' motivation and behaviour;

> considered how these various theories might support or appear contradictory to one another, and how the teacher must weigh each situation.

Branching options

The following three options are designed to provide you with additional opportunities for reflection, analysis and research. You may choose the option which best supports your currently identified needs, as set out, for example, in your action plan for a teaching qualification or for your continuing professional development (CPD). Alternatively, you may choose to work through two or even all three tasks.

1. *Reflection*
   - Take some time to reflect on your teaching over the past week. What sort of strategies or tactics have you used when addressing issues about learners' behaviour?
   - Now consider how far these are compatible with the approaches suggested by the theories of learning and motivation we've looked at in this chapter. Do you tend to use one approach more than another (for example, a Neo-behaviourist approach based on reinforcement rather than a Humanist approach based on relationship)? Are you limited in any way by your subject?
   - If there's an approach you haven't really tried yet, consider how you might incorporate it into your current professional practice.

2. *Analysis*
   - Take one recent incident over a learner's behaviour or motivation and apply to it the three main theories we've looked at here. What tactics would each theory suggest you use, in practical terms? Think about how the scenario might develop in each case, and then consider, theoretically, which you think stands the best chance of working effectively, and why.
   - If this exercise has provided you with ideas for new strategies, try implementing one of them in your next lesson.

3. *Research*
   - We've looked briefly at learning theories here, and only from the point of view of how they help us to understand learner behaviour and motivation. In order to gain a broader understanding of theory and how it can be useful to the teacher, use the internet or library facilities to find out about other learning theories, such as the *Cognitivists* and the *Gestaltists*, and theories about *Multiple Intelligences*.
   - In what ways can you apply what you've learnt from this research to the teaching of your own subject and to your own practice in motivating learners and managing their behaviour?

REFERENCES AND FURTHER READING REFERENCES AND FURTHER READING

DfES (2006) *FE Reform: Raising Skills, Improving Life Chances*. Norwich: TSO.

Foster, A. et al (2005) *Realising the Potential: A Review of the Future Role of Further Education Colleges*. Annesley: DfES.

Maslow, A. (1987) *Motivation and Personality*. New York: Harper and Row.

Rogers, C. (1983) *Freedom to Learn for the 80s*. Columbus, OH: Merrill.

Skinner, B.F. (1938) *The Behaviour of Organisms. An Experimental Analysis*. New York: D. Appleton-Century Company.

If you want a more detailed overview of learning theory than I have given here, you can find out more in, for example:

Wallace, S. (2011) *Teaching, Tutoring and Training in the Lifelong Learning Sector*, 4th edition. Exeter: Learning Matters.

8
Adult behaviour

I'm Ok, You're Ok.
Thomas A. Harris, 2012

The objectives of this chapter

This chapter looks at the needs and characteristics of adult learners in FE and discusses what these require of the teacher in terms of planning and supporting learning and of establishing positive classroom relationships. It also explores the contribution adult learners can make to the learning experience by sharing their own knowledge, skills and ideas; and stresses the need for the teacher to acknowledge these attributes and life experiences.

Introduction

So far in this book we've met a number of adult learners and discussed the challenges and opportunities they present to the teachers who are working with them. There was Tony whom we encountered in Chapter 3, who felt that his existing abilities and accomplishments were not being acknowledged. In the same chapter we discussed the cases of Rina and Sarah whose previous experience of teachers and learning had left them anxious and defensive, and whose busy adult lives were burdened with competing priorities and commitments. And then, in Chapter 7, we found poor Patrick struggling with the question of how to address the negative behaviour of one of his adult learners, Charmaine, and how to establish a positive working relationship with her. In this chapter we are going to pull all these themes together and examine in more detail the specific needs of adult learners. We recognise, from the cases we've already seen, that adults can present with difficult, negative or challenging behaviour, just as younger learners can. But the reasons for this – the issues that drive this behaviour in adults – may be rather different; and understanding these reasons is important if we're to succeed in helping them. So we'll be looking at some of the common characteristics, needs and attributes of adult FE learners and exploring their implications for good classroom practice.

The adult returner

It would be easy to assume that adult students in FE will be confident, self-assured, well-motivated learners; and people may react with disbelief if you tell them otherwise. However, we've seen already that this is often not the case. Many adults re-entering education and training through the FE sector do so because their earlier attempts at gaining useful qualifications have ended in failure and defeat. This may leave them, as in the case of Rina and Sarah, with preconceived ideas about the classroom being a place of personal humiliation, or about teachers being negative, dismissive or just plain scary. For these adult returners, stepping back into a learning environment may be a terrifying prospect, one that takes all their strength of purpose. They may arrive in your classroom feeling defensive or inadequate or convinced that it will all go wrong. But, being adults, they may be quite skilled in hiding this. Behind an apparently cheerful face someone may be thinking, *What if everyone else knows stuff I don't know? What if I get asked something and look stupid? What if this is going to be like school all over again?* Behind a carefully assumed bravado someone else may be asking themselves, *What if everyone else here is clever except for me?*

We know from previous chapters that such doubts and lack of confidence can lead to avoidance tactics, disengagement or disruption – anything to avoid having to do a task which may expose that individual's lack of knowledge or skill. And this is as true of adult learners as it is of learners in their teens. The problem is, of course, that challenging and dealing with such behaviours in an adult who is your own age or older becomes more complicated than managing a similar situation with a 16-year-old. Certainly, you are still the teacher and you are therefore 'in charge'; but there are subtleties of status, social expectation and convention at play in the power relationship between two adults, which require that you proceed with caution. Just keep in mind the story of Patrick and Charmaine in Chapter 7 as a cautionary tale. The most important thing to remember, however, is:

> The adult learner may well be feeling more vulnerable and less confident than they appear to be.

Communicating adult to adult

What we need to aim for, therefore, in all our interactions with adult learners is to keep our communication with them on an adult-to-adult basis. Now this might sound all too obvious; but it is not as straightforward to achieve this as it might seem. When we have our teacher hat on, it is all too easy to find ourselves adopting a teacherly or parental tone, especially if the majority of the classes we teach are made up of younger learners. If we adopt a parental tone or attitude when we are communicating with learners, we risk casting them into the role of 'child', which they play up to by displaying behaviour that is needy, dependent, unruly, uncooperative or any of the other types of behaviour we associate with youngsters who are being 'told off'. The psychologist, Eric Berne, explains the importance of adult-to-adult communication in his work on *Transactional Analysis* (sometimes abbreviated to TA). It is a theory well worth our consideration as educators; and one which we can easily put into practice to see the results for ourselves. Put very simply, what Berne tells us is that when we are communicating with others we adopt one of three modes of relating: as Child, Parent or Adult. If we adopt the Child mode we're likely to get a parental response from the person we're talking to. This might be exactly what we want, of course; and we can see ourselves and others using this – probably quite unconsciously – when we want a bit of sympathy or comfort. We can see adult learners going into needy Child mode when they want you to be 'Mummy' or 'Daddy' rather than requiring something too difficult from them. But Child mode also can also include loss of temper, being irrational and unreasonable, sulking, being obstructive, and so on. And this, too, brings out the Parent response in us; probably not the kind, reassuring parent this time, but the finger-wagging, stern, disapproving parent. These sorts of interactions are non-productive and can, over time, become negative and destructive. What Berne argues is that if we want our relationships to be positive and productive – in any context, not just the classroom – we need to establish the Adult to Adult model of interaction. No playing games. No manipulation or emotional blackmail. No power play. No loss of temper or snapping and sniping. Just straightforward communication, adult to adult. The reason that this is much more difficult to establish with our learners than it sounds is that we only have control, initially, over our own mode of interaction. However, if the teacher can take and maintain the approach of one reasonable adult speaking to another, there is a very good chance that, in time, the learner or learners will relinquish the Child mode (or Parent mode) because it's not getting them the response they need to keep it going.

If you go back to the story of Patrick and Charmaine in Chapter 7 you can see clearly how Charmaine reacts to what she perceives as Patrick's 'strict Parent' approach by falling straight into petulant Child mode. And then, still in Child mode, she goes to the Head of Department to try to get Patrick into trouble, seeking sympathy as a child might from 'Daddy'. She may well be one of those people who find it difficult to access her inner Adult at all. We've all met them, I guess. And, if so, she's going to be a challenge for Patrick. But then a good FE teacher is never afraid of a challenge.

CLOSE FOCUS CLOSE FOCUS CLOSE FOCUS CLOSE FOCUS CLOSE FOCUS **CLOSE FOCUS**

Consider the following interactions and see whether you can think of examples of these that you've seen or experienced in your own professional practice. How would you categorise them according to the Parent, Child, Adult modes of interacting?

1. An adult learner asks to leave the class early because he has to take his child to the dentist. The teacher tells him he should make dental appointments outside college time. The learner packs up his laptop and leaves.

2. A teacher suggests that the group of adult learners might like to help her move the tables to make one large table because this will feel more appropriate than sitting in rows. One learner folds his arms and says he hasn't come to college to move furniture. The teacher tells him she quite understands and that of course he doesn't have to help if he doesn't want to. After a moment or two he gets up and starts helping.

3. A teacher is trying to set up the data projector before class begins. An adult learner who has arrived early stands at his elbow repeatedly asking questions about last week's work. Exasperated, the teacher finally says, 'Look. Can this wait?' The learner sits down but refuses to answer any questions during the lesson.

4. A group of adult learners have been giving the trainee teacher a bad time. She walks out in the middle of a lesson and goes to see her mentor and tells him she doesn't want to teach them any more. She says, 'They're horrible and I hate them.' Her mentor tells her she's being silly and unprofessional. So she goes to see her tutor and complains that her mentor isn't up to the job.

Discussion

Hopefully all that wasn't happening on the same day at the same college.

1. In the first scenario the adult learner makes a reasonable request. He seems to be speaking here as Adult. The teacher, however, instead of responding as Adult, goes straight into Parent, admonishing him and laying down the law. As usually happens when Parent begins wagging his finger, this brings out the Child in the other who, in this case, picks up his toys and goes home.

2. In scenario 2 the teacher is communicating in Adult mode. The grumpy learner tries out his Child mode, but the teacher resists going into Parent. Instead, she keeps the interaction Adult to Adult, bringing out – eventually – an Adult response in the learner.

3. In the third scenario we see both teacher and learner in Child mode. The learner is behaving in a needy and insensitive way, demanding the teacher's attention regardless of the fact he can see that he's trying to get set up for the lesson. Instead of responding as Adult, the teacher reacts crossly, venting his feelings in an uncontrolled way typical of Child mode. There were plenty of alternative, kinder ways he could have handled this. The learner's reaction is to 'get his own back', still firmly in Child mode. This is just stacking up trouble for the teacher in future lessons.

4. In scenario 4 we see a trainee teacher reduced to Child mode (something that can easily happen when we're upset). Her Child triggers the mentor's Parent, but not exactly the response she wanted because her mentor goes into cross Parent instead of kind Parent, and so the trainee teacher takes herself off to her tutor and tries out her Child on her instead, at the same time hoping to get the mentor into trouble. Let's hope the tutor, unlike the mentor, is able to respond as Adult.

What you can see clearly from these is how an Adult response in each case would have the potential to avoid a world of trouble, as it does in Scenario 2.

Adult goals, responsibilities and expectations

As we've already seen, adult learners are usually very clear about what they want from their FE experience. Returning to learning can be a big decision for them, often involving complications with finance, child care and other responsibilities. While younger learners may drift into FE straight from school, the adult's entry into college may represent something radically different from what they've been doing previously. This can raise questions for them not just of role and identity, but also of whether they have made the best decision for themselves and their families: whether what they are getting out of it is worth the investment of their time and energy, and – for those who are paying fees – whether they are getting their money's worth. Adults, then, will have certain expectations, which you, as teacher, will need to keep in mind.

Adults are busy people and won't want to feel that any of their time is being wasted.

This means:

- always starting lessons on time;
- not finishing early (this doesn't mean that no one leaves early. You may need to be flexible over, for example, their child care arrangements);
- keeping order in the classroom. If anyone is disrupting the learning of others, this needs to be dealt with promptly, using strategies we've already discussed;
- when planning your lessons make sure you keep up plenty of pace. Adults will need to see their time being used well. This may mean having plenty of teacher input, more guided discussion and debate, less emphasis on lengthy sessions of discovery learning than you might find useful with younger learners.

Adults have complicated lives and multiple responsibilities.

This means:

- they need accurate and reliable information about their timetable. So give them a timetable and make sure you stick to it. There may be sessions they will have to miss because of other responsibilities. They need to know exactly what's coming up so that they can plan ahead.

Adults need to feel a sense of ownership over their own learning.

This means:

- they need to know the intended learning outcomes at the beginning of each session. This provides them with a map. It lets them know where the lesson is going and helps them to add their own efforts to yours in achieving those goals. And review the outcomes at the end of the session so that you can reach some agreement on whether or to what extent they've been achieved. This acknowledges the adult's stake in their own learning. This also creates a sense of order, which makes it easier for them to catch up on any session they miss.

Adults' time for working on assignments will be precious time they take away from their family and other responsibilities, so they need to know very clearly what is expected of them.

This means:

- you must make sure that they have clear information about the assessment criteria that will be used in marking any work they are required to do. You should at all costs avoid 'ambush assessment'; that is, setting a piece of work without giving any clear idea of what criteria you will apply in marking it. Will they be penalised for spelling or grammatical errors, for example? Can they present their work in bullet points? Must they hand in hard copy or can they submit via the VLE? They may not want to ask these questions for fear of embarrassment, so you will need to think ahead about what information they need.

All of these are ways you can plan ahead to avoid conflict and difficulties arising with your adult learners. Careful planning is often the best answer. Keeping the learners well motivated and positively engaged from the start is far preferable to having to rescue difficult situations in order to rebuild trust and harmony.

Ade goes back to college

Following repeated periods of unemployment, Ade decides to try and get some qualifications which will give him a competitive edge in the job market. Now in his forties, he went into his first job straight from school, loading vans for a local beer wholesaler. Since then he has had a number of unskilled jobs, none of which has lasted more than a year or two. His GCSE results were poor and he didn't get either maths or English. He has come into college on a skills for work programme, having been told he can progress from this on to a specific vocational skills course. Some of the skills for work curriculum involves basic English and maths, and Ade is finding that this reminds him a little too much of school.

TASK TASK TASK **TASK** TASK TASK **TASK** TASK TASK **TASK** TASK TASK

Read the following account of an incident between Ade and one of his teachers, Gina, and consider the following questions.

1. What went wrong here, and why?

2. Could this have been avoided, and if so, how?

3. If Gina came to you for advice, what would you say to her?

4. Do you think there is anything about this incident that might have happened differently if Gina had been dealing with a younger learner?

Gina is teaching a communication lesson on the skills for work programme. She has planned the lesson around looking at the way advertisers use language to convince and persuade. Her aim is to help the learners understand that communication can be used in different ways according to our purpose. After showing and discussing a selection of adverts via the data projector, she gives out some glossy magazine adverts and asks the learners to discuss these in small groups and decide which are most persuasive and why. At this point Ade pushes back his chair and announces that he is going home. Everyone stops what they're doing to look at him. Then they look at Gina. How is she going to respond to this? Here's how the conversation goes:

Gina: *Where are you going, Ade?*

Ade: (walking towards the door) *I've just said. Home.*

Gina: *No. Come back. You can't do that.*

Ade: *Can't do that? What do you mean, can't do that?*

Gina: *You can't just leave in the middle of the lesson. Ade, come back! Just tell me what's the matter.*

Ade: (stopping by the door and turning round). *Right. I'll tell you what's the matter. You're wasting my time, that's what's the matter. You're wasting my time with looking at bloody adverts. What's this got to do with finding a job? Nothing! I can't ever afford most of this stuff you're showing us. Even if I get work, right? And how is this going to get me into work? I take two buses to get here and two buses to get home. I've got the neighbour meeting the kids from school. And all just to come here and look at bloody adverts. I see enough of this rubbish at home.*

Gina: *But Ade, you're missing the point...*

Ade: *Am I? Well, I'll tell you what. I'm not going to miss my bus.*

He leaves and slams the door behind him.

Discussion

1. What went wrong here, and why?

Leaving aside for a moment the question of whether Gina made a wise choice with this particular topic, we can see that her initial response to Ade ('Where are you going?') was firmly in Parent mode. This simply reinforces Ade in his role as cross child. We can understand Gina asking this question. It was probably a knee-jerk response. But to an angry adult its accusatory tone acts like a red rag to a bull. And she doesn't pick up on this or learn from it because she's still *responding to Ade in bossy Parent mode* right to the end, telling him he's 'missed the point'. Up to this moment she could perhaps have rescued the situation, but her final comment is clearly the last straw for Ade.

2. Could this have been avoided, and if so, how?

There are several ways all this could have been avoided. Gina could have been more sensitive in her choice of resources. If the topic was use of language, why didn't she look at the language of job ads, for example, or base the lesson around how to write a persuasive job application – something where the *relevance to the learners' goals* was clear? She could also have responded to Ade's declared intention to leave in a way that *kept the interaction on an adult-to-adult level*. She could have said, 'Let me walk out with you, Ade' and then listened to his complaint quietly in the corridor rather than in view of all the other learners. She could have acknowledged, adult-to-adult, that she understood the point he was making, and assured him that she would bear it mind when planning future sessions.

3. If Gina came to you for advice, what would you say to her?

You'd probably advise her to be more sensitive to the circumstances of her adult learners; to keep in mind the fact that bombarding them with adverts for shiny consumer goods could have the effect of reinforcing their sense of failure at being out of work. You'd also advise her that, with busy lives and complex commitments, these adult learners need to see the direct relevance to their own goals and aspirations of anything and everything you are teaching them. You'd remind her to keep all her interactions with these learners on an adult-to-adult level and at all costs avoid triggering a Child response in them by taking on for yourself the role of stern or bossy Parent. You would also suggest to her that she avoids 'performing' confrontations of any kind in front of the whole class, as this can be humiliating for teacher and learner alike.

4. Do you think there is anything about this incident that might have happened differently if Gina had been dealing with a younger learner?

This is a tricky one. Everything we've said so far in this discussion could also usefully apply to younger learners. It is just possible that a younger learner might not have responded so indignantly to being asked where he was going. Being addressed by teachers in stern Parent mode might be almost an expectation to someone recently out of school. But that wouldn't necessarily make it right.

Using learner experience as your best resource

Finally, a word about adult learners as a resource. This is an aspect of working with adults that teachers can often forget or overlook. Adult learners arrive in FE with a varied and often rich set of life experiences. These may be to do with aspects of the world of work or of family life and relationships; or they may be to do with places they have travelled to or books they have read or people they have met. For younger teachers, and particularly younger trainee teachers, this very fact can seem at first threatening. *'What if they know more than I do?'* or *'What if they ask me something and I don't know the answer?'* If you have ever asked yourself these questions it may reassure you to know that these are common worries for teachers just starting out on their professional involvement with adult learning. And the answer to both questions is very simple: It doesn't matter. In fact it can be used to enrich and enliven your teaching. If a learner has expertise in a curriculum subject, draw on that. Acknowledge it. Say, 'Tony, you had some experience of survey methods when you were in the army. Can you tell us a bit about that?' And if Tony goes on to ask you a question you don't know the answer to, you respond, adult-to-adult: 'I don't know. Let's make a point of looking that one up before the next lesson.' It's ok to not know everything. That's what the internet is for. And it's ok for learners to know more than you do sometimes, if their life experience has already equipped them with that knowledge. Think back to Tony in Chapter 3, whose sense of identity was becoming undermined by the failure of his FE teachers to acknowledge his life experiences and achievements. When you recognise and draw on your adult learners' knowledge you are demonstrating respect, building their confidence and establishing a positive working relationship. Of course, you can only do this if you take the time to get to know them and learn something of the trajectory that brought them into FE and back into learning.

A SUMMARY OF KEY POINTS A SUMMARY OF KEY POINTS A SUMMARY OF KEY POINTS

In this chapter we have:

> discussed some of the characteristics of adult learners, emphasising the point that adult returners may feel more vulnerable and less confident than they appear to be;

> considered the importance of adult-to-adult communication, using Berne's concept of Transactional Analysis;

> set out practical ways in which we as teachers can take into account adult learners' goals, responsibilities and expectations.

> looked at how we can use adults' expertise and life experience as a positive resource in supporting their learning.

Branching options

The following three options are designed to provide you with additional opportunities for reflection, analysis and research. You may choose the option which best supports your currently identified needs; or you may find it useful to work through all three tasks.

1. *Reflection*
   - Think about a group of adults you have taught or one that you have observed being taught by a colleague or mentor. Did their behaviour or attitude differ in any way from that of younger learners you've taught? If so, in what ways?
   - When you are planning lessons for adults, do you do anything differently from your planning for younger learners? If you've never produced a lesson plan for adult learners, ask your mentor this question and discuss the answer with him/her.
   - Does your manner of communicating with the adults at work – learners or colleagues – differ from the way you speak to younger learners? Observe your own interactions for a day and then reflect on this.

2. *Analysis*
   - If you are reading this book as part of your initial teacher training or CPD, you yourself fall into the category of adult learner. Which of the characteristics of adult learners discussed in this chapter do you recognise in yourself?
   - Look back at previous chapters and re-read the stories of Rina and Sarah and of Tony (all in Chapter 3) and of Charmaine (Chapter 7), and analyse these in terms of what you have learnt from this chapter. What issues are driving their behaviour? What strategies could be used to help them?

3. *Research*
   - Ask some of the adult learners at your college why they have returned to learning. How can you make use of what they tell you in your own practice?
   - Access one of the texts cited at the end of this chapter, either through the internet or with the help of your college librarian. Choose a chapter to read. What further insights does it provide?

REFERENCES AND FURTHER READING REFERENCES AND FURTHER READING

Harris, T. A. (2012) *I'm Ok, You're Ok (A Practical Guide to Transactional Analysis)*. New York: Arrow Books.

Rogers, A. and Horrocks, N. (2010) *Teaching Adults*, 4th edition. Maidenhead: Open University Press.

Stewart, I. and Joines, V. (2012) *Transactional Analysis Today: A New Introduction to Transactional Analysis*, 2nd edition. Chapel Hill, NC: Lifespace Publishing.

9
The Young Ones

Crabbed age and youth cannot live together;
Youth is full of pleasance, age is full of care.
Shakespeare, *The Passionate Pilgrim*

The objectives of this chapter

This chapter looks at the needs and characteristics of 14–16-year-old learners who follow a vocational programme in FE as an alternative to part or all of the Key Stage 4 school curriculum. It offers some practical strategies for motivating and engaging younger learners, and encourages you to reflect on ways in which your lesson planning and teaching style can be tailored to meet their needs.

Introduction

Working with younger learners can be unfamiliar territory even for experienced FE teachers. We tend to think of FE learners as falling into the category of 16+ school leavers or adults aged 19 and over. Our lesson planning strategies and repertoire of teaching methods will have been developed primarily with these two groups in mind. It's possible, therefore, that finding ourselves timetabled to teach 14–16-year-olds is going to nudge us out of our safety zone. There's nothing wrong with that. Taking on a professional challenge is a good thing, as long as we're adequately prepared. What we don't want is to be feeling too anxious about it, because if we don't appear comfortable or confident, learners can pick up on this and find it unsettling. So this is going to be a chapter with lots of practical suggestions for those who haven't taught this age group before. But first we're going to take a look at one teacher's initial experiences of working with younger learners.

Dara and the young ones

Dara is in his first year of teaching in FE and hasn't taught younger learners before. He is quite apprehensive when he sees that his timetable includes two 2-hour sessions a week with 14–15-year-old learners who will be spending part of their school week on a vocational programme at college which will replace part of their national curriculum requirement. However, after his first session with them he feels a bit more confident. His good-natured approach and sense of humour seem to have gone down well and the learners appear to be responding positively to him. Consequently he feels a bit more relaxed about the second session of the week and – being rushed off his feet in this first week of full-time teaching – he doesn't spend quite as long as he would otherwise have done over planning his lesson with them.

TASK TASK TASK **TASK** TASK TASK **TASK** TASK TASK **TASK** TASK TASK

Read the account of Dara's second session with the young learners and consider the following questions:

- **How does Dara initially establish order in the workshop? What are the stages by which he does this? Look carefully at the strategies he uses. Which ones work best, and why? What alternative or additional strategies might you have used if you were in his place?**

- **What strategies does Dara use to maintain a positive working relationship with this class and to motivate them?**

- **Writing their comments up on the whiteboard was clearly not part of his original lesson plan. So why do you think he decides to do this? What was his purpose? Did it succeed?**

- **He seemed to be doing okay; so what went wrong at the end? Where did it *begin* to go wrong? What could he have done differently?**

- **Given the situation he now finds himself in, how would you advise him to proceed?**

Dara arrives in the workshop a little late because his previous lesson over-ran. He enters to a barrage of noise. Some of the learners are racing about the room, laughing and yelling. Others are shouting over them and seem to be throwing something about. And there's music playing very loudly, although Dara can't, at first sight, see where it's coming from. He slams his files down hard on the front bench to get their attention, but no one takes any notice. So he claps his hands together loudly and shouts, 'Okay. Come on. Settle down now.' This, too, has little effect. He's spotted where the music is coming from, now, rigged to one of the workshop's speaker systems. He goes over and turns it off. This is greeted by groans, but at least he has their attention. 'Don't worry,' he says. 'I'm going to put this back on as soon as we've covered all learning outcomes for this lesson. So the better you listen and the harder you work, the more time you'll get to hear this at the end. Come on, sit down now.'

Most of them do. But two boys are still racing around. They look as though they're playing tag. He points to them and says to the rest of class, 'But that's not going to help, is it?' The other learners start urging the racing boys to stop it and sit down. Eventually they do that, and Dara is able to begin the lesson. He starts by asking a few questions about what they learnt in their previous lesson with him. No one volunteers an answer. He then picks on a couple of learners by name, but they've no answers for him either. He feels discouraged, because he'd thought the previous lesson went well. Exasperated, he says, 'So are you telling me that *no one* remembers what we did last time?'

'It was boring, wasn't it?' says one of the boys who'd been running round.

'Yeah,' says another. 'It was well boring. Why can't we do something interesting?'

'Well, I'm sorry you thought it was boring,' says Dara. 'I thought it was fantastic.'

This gets a laugh. Dara tries to explain that before they can get on to the 'interesting' stuff – by which he assumes they mean hands-on practical work – they have to know what they're doing and why; and they have to understand about safety issues.

'But it's not supposed to be all talking,' says one of the girls. 'That's like school, that is. School's all talking. I'd have stayed at school if I wanted all talking, right?'

The rest of the class voice their general assent to this. Dara is aware of them all watching him, waiting to see how he'll respond. He nods to signal his agreement. 'Tell me about it then,' he

▶

says. 'Tell me what you were expecting when you came here. No. One at a time. I'm going to put what you say up on the whiteboard so that we can have a look at it and see if we can come up with a plan.'

He writes up their comments. Most of them are about wanting a learning experience that is completely different from school; expecting to engage in practical tasks; expecting to get some understanding of the world of work; being treated like adults. Some of the comments are flippant or silly, but he writes those up, too and the learners laugh at them. He feels as though he has achieved a change of mood in the class. It all feels good-natured and cooperative and positive.

He goes through the points they have made, one by one, and explains that – really, if they think about it – this is what he's been doing with them already. All of this. So why don't they all get on now and have a look together at the objectives for today's lesson.

'Can we have a break first?' asks the girl who thought school was about being talked at.

They all begin to chime in. Yes, they want a break. The other teacher always lets them have a break. And after the break can they have the music back on? He said they could have it back on.

'No,' says Dara. 'I didn't. And you can't have a break. There's no scheduled break. And anyway, you haven't done any work yet.'

'What's that, then?' demands the girl, pointing at the whiteboard.

'That's not work,' says Dara.

'Well, what you wasting our time with it for, then?' she says.

Discussion

In discussing the task, let's take our questions one at a time.

1. First, how does Dara initially establish order in the workshop?

Well, he does this in stages. His first attempt – banging the files on the desk – doesn't accomplish much. What's more, it could look to the learners as though he's expressing anger or frustration, which, as we've seen in previous chapters, is unlikely to lead anywhere positive. Luckily, they don't seem even to notice this gesture, so he's able to proceed to more positive strategies. He tries clapping his hands and calling for order. This doesn't have much effect either. It's when he goes over and turns the music off that he gets their attention. By this time he's thinking more creatively about his strategy. Instead of getting cross with the learners, he promises them they'll have music again when they've done some work. This positive approach and promise of reward works well at settling them down. He then uses a cunning strategy to call the two running boys to order: he sets up peer pressure. There'll be no more music until the work is done. The work won't get done while these two are running about. So therefore he can stand back and let the rest of the class, in their own best interests, call the boys to order. We can summarise his approach like this:

- **Promises reward rather than threatens punishment.**
- **Avoids direct confrontation and commands.**
- **Sets up a situation that employs peer pressure rather than teacher authority.**

This was not the only way he could have addressed the situation, and you may prefer to use different strategies. What's important here is that you see why his first two strategies worked and his second two didn't.

2. What strategies does Dara use to maintain a positive working relationship with this class and to motivate them?

Having effectively established some sort of order, Dara must now find ways to maintain this. He's already used as a motivator the promise of music in return for work completed. But he needs to keep the motivation going. One of the things he does is to use humour. He makes them laugh; he keeps his relationship with them positive, even though they are complaining. He writes their views on the whiteboard, demonstrating that he values what they have to say and is willing to listen. He tells them that they will come up with a plan together, signalling that he is prepared to negotiate a way forward. He even records the 'flippant or silly' comments, again avoiding direct confrontation and power-play and showing up the silliness for what it is. All of this demonstrates to the learners that he values their opinions and that they are working together with a shared purpose. It's designed to build learners' self-esteem and sense of self-advocacy. All of this seems to work well initially in terms of improving motivation and creating a positive atmosphere. His attempts to explain how his work with them is already fulfilling these items on their wish list goes down less well. This explanation was also obviously an attempt at motivating and engaging them, but it doesn't seem to work, and you might like to consider why this could be.

3. Writing their comments up on the whiteboard was clearly not part of his original lesson plan. So why do you think he decides to do this? What was his purpose?

We've already partially answered this question in answering the one before. It was about building a sense of self-advocacy and demonstrating that he values their views. But his purpose also seems to have been to use the list to show them that his lessons with them are already meeting some of their expectations. This was quite a high-risk strategy, and it doesn't seem to succeed. This may be because the learners felt they'd been tricked or backed into a corner. Or it may be because they had engaged enthusiastically with making the list only to avoid getting down to work, and that avoiding getting down to work is their main concern all along.

4. What went wrong at the end?

Well, if the learners don't want to work, they'll resist even the most good-natured efforts to engage them. And Dara's plan does seem to go wrong at the point where he uses their own comments to explain how he is right and that they should therefore get on with the tasks he's planned for them. It's difficult to say what he could have done differently at this point. Perhaps he could have continued to negotiate – invite them to suggest some of the lesson content, for example. They obviously want to get 'hands on', and it's difficult to see why he keeps resisting this. However, if the main driver here is the learners' determination to avoid getting down to work, we need to unpack this a little further. They are new to FE. They are younger than most of the other learners. They're little fish in a big pond, and they may feel that being here is somehow a consequence of failure, in that they're not expected to achieve well in Key Stage 4. So they may well be scared to engage with the work. They may be asking themselves, *what if they can't cope with this either? What then?* So they ask for a break and start another argument. Dara should recognise these as classic avoidance tactics.

5. Given the situation he now finds himself in, how would you advise him to proceed?

It may be that what these learners need is not so much explanation of why Dara is right as reassurance that the lesson he's planned will involve nothing they can't cope with. Perhaps he needs to talk them through what's going to happen in the lesson, allow some time for questions before they begin, and build their confidence that they'll be able to do it.

Some characteristics of 14–16-year-olds in FE

So, bearing Dara's story in mind, can we say that there are any particular characteristics that differentiate 14-year-old learners from those who are a few years older? I'm going to suggest that there are. You may want to argue, however, that some of the ones I list below can apply equally to learners of all ages, and you could be right. What is important is that you consider this list in the light of your own experiences and observations.

- **Younger learners may find the FE environment intimidating and their fear may create a barrier to their learning.**
- **They may find it difficult to adapt to the freedoms which FE allows them in comparison to school, and respond by behaving inappropriately.**
- **They may have a shorter attention span than older learners.**
- **They may be unused to taking responsibility for their own learning and may therefore be unable to do so.**
- **They may be restless and find it difficult to sit still for any period of time.**
- **They may, as a result of being directed away from school and onto a vocational route, see themselves in some sense as 'failures'.**
- **By definition, their experience of school may not have been a positive one and this may have caused them to be resistant to learning.**
- **By the same principle, they may see teachers as 'the enemy' and arrive at college predisposed to dislike and distrust you.**
- **On the other hand, they may have great expectations that FE and FE teachers are going to be the answer to all their problems, and be disappointed when they find that rules and the need for a co-operative attitude still apply as they did at school.**
- **Or – and let's not forget this one – they may find that FE is indeed everything they hoped it would be, and find the inner motivation to work hard and succeed with their learning. But, as this is a book about supporting learners who don't quite fall into this category yet, we'll just acknowledge these well-motivated ones here and move on.**

These are generalisations, of course. But it's useful to reflect on them because there's the possibility they can give us a 'handle' on what's going on with younger learners' behaviour and why. They also help us to identify a set of needs, which may help us with our lesson planning. These can be summarised as the need for:

- **structure, security and routine;**
- **plenty of opportunities for activity;**
- **a sense of vocational relevance and purpose;**
- **opportunities to build their self-esteem and sense of belonging;**
- **opportunities to reward them;**
- **clarity of communication, including step-by-step instruction;**
- **making learning a positive experience.**

You can see at once how each of these relates to the humanist or Neo-behaviourist theories of motivation that we looked at in Chapter 7, and particularly to Maslow's proposition that our needs for safety, self-esteem and belonging need to be met before we can attend to the business of learning.

Now let's take each point listed above and explore what it means in terms of practical strategies that you can employ in your planning and your teaching.

Building in structure, security and routine

College can at first seem a much less structured environment than school; and this contrast is particularly apparent to 14–16-year-old learners who may be spending part of the week in each. This can create the temptation to test boundaries but can also trigger insecurities and anxieties. We saw a bit of both with Dara's class. First, they run riot; then they try every tactic they can to avoid the scary business of college-level learning. Providing structure and routine is one way to address this. For example, you could try the following strategies:

- At a classroom level you can provide structure by ensuring that your lessons always follow a pattern which the learners can quickly become familiar with. This doesn't mean implementing the same activities every time – far from it. It means things such as always (and therefore reliably) making a prompt start and finishing on time; always beginning with a recap of the previous lesson and moving on to a clear explanation of the learning objectives for this one; building in a question and answer session at the same point in the lesson; and so on.
- Providing security and routine also means ensuring your own behaviour is consistent and your treatment of the learners is fair. Don't unnerve them with unsettling mood swings, an unpredictable temper or obvious shows of favouritism.
- Make sure you tell learners what they are going to be doing at the beginning of each lesson; make sure they do it; and then, at the end, remind them of what they've done.
- It can be a good idea to start each lesson with a settling activity such as a brief quiz or puzzle of some kind that can act as a recap to the last lesson and a preface to this one. If you make it something fun and brief, learners will settle down to it readily.
- Give clear guidance on time limits for tasks. Tell them, 'You've got ten minutes to complete this.' Give them a five-minute warning, a three-minute warning and a one-minute warning. Make sure they all stop when you tell them to. As well as providing time boundaries, this strategy also helps keep up the pace and injects a sense of competition, which makes it fun, even if it's only against the clock.
- Make your own boundaries clear by setting out your own rules for classroom behaviour. Or, better still, agree a set of rules that the learners can feel some ownership of. And then make sure they're applied, consistently and fairly.
- To establish a sense of structure at the college level, it's a good idea to go through the college rules with them, emphasising the principles of respect and inclusion.
- And make sure you stick to those college rules yourself and don't belittle or criticise any particular rule, otherwise you're giving the learners mixed messages.

Creating opportunities for activity

Because younger learners can be restless and full of energy, and because their attention span can be shorter than that of older learners, it's important to build the following into your lesson plans:

- Plenty of active participative learning. We saw how Dara's learners were impatient for some hands-on learning; but learners won't necessarily articulate this need as clearly as they did. They may communicate it instead by fooling about or refusing to engage. So we need always to keep in mind the possibilities of kinaesthetic learning – that is, learning through physical activity – and also the difficulty that younger learners may have in sitting still and simply listening. Only a minority of people, whatever their age, learn best like that. You might try, for example, strategies like using a sponge ball (or something else non-hazardous) in question and answer sessions, throwing it to the learner who's volunteering an answer by putting up a hand for it; or allowing learners to nominate someone to answer by throwing the ball to them. This incorporates activity and fun into what would otherwise be simply cognitive learning.

- Frequent changes of activity to accommodate those shorter attention spans. Younger learners become easily bored. A range of short, well-paced learning activities will normally keep them engaged more effectively than one activity which goes on for a long time.
- Frequent breaks. These needn't be scheduled breaks. There are obviously health and safety issues about letting learners out of the classroom or workshop while they are formally under your supervision. However, a 'break' may simply be an opportunity for the learners to stand up and stretch; or three minutes of Check Your Texts time; or three minutes of Talk to Your Neighbour time. The advantage of these strategies is that they can also be offered as a reward for completion of tasks. 'When everyone's finished this, we're going to have three minutes of Check Your Texts time.' This sort of reward can be a very effective motivator.

Creating a sense of vocational relevance and purpose

The reason that most 14- and 15-year-olds are in FE is because it's believed that they will find the vocational curriculum more suited to their interests than the academic school curriculum. It's very important always to keep this in mind. Use of the vocational context can be a very useful motivator. This can include the following strategies:

- Emphasise your own vocational credentials. Use opportunities to remind them – positively – that you have experience at doing the work they are aspiring to, and that therefore you know what you're talking about.
- Relate each new learning activity to the work context. For example, you might tell them, *'When you're doing this for real in a couple of years' time you'll probably find you get treated as the expert.'* Or, *'When you're doing this procedure in the workplace you'll probably need to...'* And so on.
- Relate behaviour issues to the work context. *'What might happen if you waved that around like that on site?'* Or, *'What would be the health and safety issues if you were to do that at work?'* Or, *'Think about how you would need to talk to a customer. Let's have a go at that today.'* If you are negotiating rules of behaviour with them, point out the appropriateness of each rule to the workplace and remind them that these are the rules under which they'll eventually be operating when they're in employment.
- Select learning resources that relate directly to their chosen vocational area, whether it's pictures on the data projector, case studies to work on, or actual bits of kit they can handle. This is something that Dara could bear in mind.

Building learners' self-esteem and sense of belonging

We've already seen why some young learners may have low self-esteem and lack confidence in their own ability to cope with FE. There are lots of ways for you to address this. We saw Dara use several strategies with the group as a whole. But you can build the confidence of individual learners, too. Remember these key points:

- Look pleased to be with them.
- Show an interest in their views and their achievements (and their fashion statements and haircuts and new phones – whatever it takes).
- Praise them whenever possible. If it's difficult to praise their work, praise their behaviour. If it's difficult to praise their behaviour, find something else to praise – the fact that they're wearing regulation safety boots, for example. Praise is addictive. If the learners haven't been used to receiving praise at school they may have developed the habit of getting attention from teachers in other ways which involve negative behaviour. If they find they can get positive attention instead, in the form of praise, they may well discard old habits and come back for more. What you are doing

here is challenging the learners' belief that nothing they do in terms of education and training will be praiseworthy. That's a belief well worth challenging.

Finding ways to reward them

Praise is one of many ways to reward young learners. Dara comes up with an interesting one – the promise of music if they complete their tasks. Some FE teachers find that prizes are an effective reward, and give out sweets for correct answers or excellent work. Others consider this to be a patronising approach that infantalises the learners. But there is plenty of evidence that it can work well. We've seen already that certain activities can be used as a reward in instances where the whole group have completed a task on time or worked productively in some other way. Whole group rewards have an added advantage in that they have the potential for exerting peer pressure on reluctant or recalcitrant learners, because if even one individual doesn't get the work done, everyone loses out. Peer pressure can be a more effective motivator than teacher pressure, while at the same time keeping the learner–teacher relationship on a positive footing.

Ensuring clear communication and instruction

Clear communication is an essential part of providing structure and a sense of safety. For example, tasks should always be broken down into small steps, and instructions should be clear and repeated as many times as is necessary. It is advisable to:

- make the objectives of a task clear. What are they expected to achieve, and why? What is its relevance to their chosen vocational area? How does it fit into their learning trajectory – what will it allow them to go on and do next?
- at the end of the task, go over this again. Explain what they have now achieved and why this was important in helping them achieve their job ambitions.
- display written instructions for each task (on whiteboard or via data projector) as well as giving them verbally. This is essential if there's a lot of noise going on in the room.
- go over the instructions in detail, step by step. Invite and answer questions. Take as long as necessary over this stage. It'll be time well invested. Don't set the learners off on the task until you're confident that they're all clear about what they have to do.
- don't just leave them to it. While they work, move about the classroom or workshop observing, advising, asking and answering questions.
- be patient. Be prepared to repeat and explain instructions as many times as it takes.
- choose your language carefully. Make sure you're using a vocabulary they understand. If a learner is having difficulty understanding, try phrasing it in a different way and/or giving some familiar concrete examples.

Making learning a positive experience

As we've already acknowledged, the previous learning experiences of some 14–16-year-olds in FE may not have been positive ones, and may have left them with a tendency to resist and distrust teachers. Some useful ways of challenging these preconceptions include:

- incorporating learning activities which are fun into your lesson plan. This might include simulations, games, quizzes, competitions, role-play, case studies and any activities that involve movement and practical work.
- demonstrating your own enthusiasm and approachability. Dara shows us that he's good at this. They can't cast you in the role of a baddy if your attitude towards them is positive and accepting.
- never, ever exposing a learner to ridicule or making them feel a failure. These younger learners are

at an age where embarrassment can be the greatest fear. Remember Maslow's hierarchy of needs. No one can learn effectively if they don't feel safe, and that especially goes for the young ones.

A SUMMARY OF KEY POINTS A SUMMARY OF KEY POINTS A SUMMARY OF KEY POINTS

In this chapter we have:

> considered some of the characteristics typical of 14–16-year-olds in FE;

> looked at some useful strategies for supporting them in their learning. This has included meeting their need for structure, security and routine; the importance of providing active learning experiences and clear vocational relevance; ways of building their self-esteem and sense of belonging; the importance of reward; and the need for clear, step-by-step instruction.

Branching options

The following three options are designed to provide you with additional opportunities for reflection, analysis and research. You may choose the option which best supports your currently identified needs; or you may find it useful to work through all three tasks.

1. *Reflection*
   - Think about a group of younger learners you have taught or one that you have observed being taught by a colleague or mentor. Did their behaviour or attitude differ in any way from that of other learners you've taught? If so, in what ways?
   - When you are planning lessons for younger learners what do you do to plan for the learning needs specifically of this age group? If you've never produced a lesson plan for younger learners, ask your mentor this question and discuss the answer with them.
   - Does your manner of communicating with younger learners differ from the way you communicate with other age groups? Observe your own interactions for a day and then reflect on this.

2. *Analysis*
   - Look again at Dara's story. Using the needs-related strategies discussed in this chapter, consider which of these he might apply to the planning of his next lesson in order to re-establish a positive working relationship with his young learners.

3. *Research*
   - Ask some of the younger learners at your college why they are in FE rather than full time at school. How can you make use of what they tell you in your own practice?
   - Use the internet to access the full text of the 2005 White Paper, *14–19 Education and Skills*, which first set out the political argument for allowing 14–16-year-olds to undertake part of their Key Stage 4 learning in FE colleges. What are the key points of this argument? To what extent are they still relevant today?

REFERENCES AND FURTHER READING REFERENCES AND FURTHER READING

Hodgson, A. and Spours, K. (2008) *Education and Training 14–19: Curriculum, Qualifications & Organisation.* London: Sage.
Pring, R. (2009) *Education for All: The Future of Education and Training for 14–19 year olds.* London: Routledge.

10
Putting the flags out

*To change your mind and to follow one who sets you right
is to be none the less the free agent that you were before.*
Marcus Aurelius AD 121–180

The objectives of this chapter

This chapter looks at ways in which teachers can motivate learners by helping them to recognise their own achievements, however small. It is about finding successes to celebrate and giving positive, constructive feedback, even in difficult circumstances. As well as examining the role that empathy and body language have to play in managing behaviour, it focuses on some of the attributes and qualities which we would expect to see in an effective teacher, and explores how these might translate into practice.

Introduction

The qualities which enable an individual to motivate and bring out the best in others are easy to recognise when we see them, but often difficult to define. If we can't define them, how do we go about fostering and developing them? This has raised the question in some minds as to whether the best teachers are born that way, or whether such skills can be taught. I think they *can* be taught; but I think that they can be best taught by example. I'm not sure anyone ever learnt to be an inspirational teacher by listening to a lecture on how to be one. One of the things we're going to do in this chapter, therefore, is to look at some examples of leadership, and see what we can learn from these about what it takes to give people confidence in themselves; to give them heart; to make them want to achieve. The first examples we'll look at will not be specifically from the world of teaching, but from other areas of leadership, because it will do us good to get out of the classroom and the workshop for a while. From these wider examples we'll be able to draw some lessons, which we can then apply to our practice as teachers, about just what it is that enables some people to bring out the best in others.

Leadership

We have seen, in Chapter 2 and Chapter 3, that there are some learners in FE who feel that there is no point in making an effort to learn because they'll gain nothing from it, however hard they try. We have also seen that there are some who, for this reason or for some other, are uncooperative and mistrustful of you, the teacher. These are the learners we want to reach; not just because it makes our life easier if they become willing learners, but because when we do reach them, and we do begin to find ways to encourage them and support their learning, we have the satisfaction of knowing we have done one of the most difficult and rewarding things a teacher can do. We have changed someone's life. We won't reach all of them, and we won't succeed every day, and perhaps not even every week; but we'll try to discover in this chapter what we can do to make this kind of success more likely.

To begin with, this is going to take us to Antarctica and the South Atlantic, and then into an open boat on the Pacific Ocean – a prospect that may come as a welcome to relief to some of us, after some of the classes we've taught this week.

In 1914 Ernest Shackleton set out with a hand-picked crew to cross the Antarctic continent – a journey of over 2000 miles. Their ship, the *Endurance*, became trapped in the Antarctic ice, which finally crushed and sank it. To get his men to safety, Shackleton led them for days across miles of disintegrating ice floes, dragging the small boats they had salvaged from the ship, and then across the open sea to the nearest dry land, Elephant Island, itself a barren, rocky waste. From there, Shackleton put to sea again in one of the little boats with a handful of the fitter men, and sailed 800 miles through the stormy seas of the South Atlantic to South Georgia from where he was able to organise a rescue. He wrote to his wife: 'Not a life lost, and we have been through hell.' His comment has become famous, summing up as it does the remarkable endurance and determination of this group of otherwise ordinary men.

Over a hundred years earlier, history tells us of another, and in some ways similar, feat of leadership. This time the man in charge navigated a small open boat almost 4000 miles across the Pacific Ocean to land safely in Java without losing a single one of his 18 men. They survived storms, starvation and attack from South Pacific Islanders; their leader took them through all of this to safety. However, he has gone down in history with a rather different reputation to that of Shackleton. His name was Captain Bligh, of the *Bounty*.

Shackleton brought his crew to safety, and in the process won their co-operation and respect. Bligh, too, brought his crew to safety, but in the process earned their loathing. They seem to have feared rather than respected him, and their co-operation was grudging, to say the least.

So, you may ask, what has this got to do with teaching in the FE sector? My answer would be that it has a lot to do with it if we are interested in how people can be encouraged and motivated; and how mutinous behaviour or loss of hope can be turned into a sense of achievement and purpose.

It's tempting to imagine that the people Shackleton was leading were a homogenous, cooperative group, and that Bligh simply had the bad luck to find himself leading a surly crew. But this was not, in fact, the case. There were objections early on to Shackleton's plan to drag the boats across the ice, and some of the men, with the ship's carpenter as their spokesperson, came very close to mutiny. So how did Shackleton maintain his leadership and keep up the group's morale so that they remained motivated and task-oriented? What were the differences in the way these two leaders behaved that produced such different responses in their crews?

TASK TASK TASK TASK TASK TASK TASK TASK TASK TASK TASK TASK

We'll have a look now at some of the things we know about how these two managed and motivated the groups in their charge. We can get some insight into this from accounts written at the time. For example, like you, Shackleton kept a journal. Bligh kept a log; and members of his crew recounted their version of events, too. Below you'll find some summaries of these accounts.

- **Read through them and identify the conclusions we might draw about what kind of leadership behaviours are likely to motivate, and what leadership behaviours would tend to have the opposite effect.**
- **How would you describe the difference between the attitude of each of these two leaders towards those in their care?**
- **What links can you make here to classroom practice?**

When they first had to abandon ship and pitch tents on the ice in −16 degrees, Shackleton tells us:

> *I mustered all hands and explained the position to them briefly and, I hope, clearly ... I stated that I propose to try to march with equipment across the ice ... I thanked the men for the steadiness and good morale they had shown in these trying circumstances, and told them I had no doubt that, provided they continued to work their utmost and to trust me, we will all reach safety in the end.*
>
> Shackleton (1999) p. 77

During the first few days cast adrift in the open boat, Bligh also made an attempt to keep up the spirits of the crew. The way he went about this was by telling them what it was going to be like when they reached the nearest land. Unfortunately, his stories of the savagery of the New Guinea inhabitants, far from entertaining the men, horrified them and made them extremely anxious.

As Shackleton leads the group across the ice, he reflects:

> *I knew how important it was to keep the men cheerful, and that the depression occasioned by our surroundings and our precarious position could to some extent be alleviated by increasing the rations ... The apathy which seemed to take possession of some of the men ... was soon dispelled. Parties were sent out daily in different directions to look for seals and penguins ... The possible number of permutations of seal meat were decidedly limited. The fact that the men did not know what [recipe] was coming gave them a sort of mental speculation, and the slightest variation was of great value.*
>
> Shackleton (1999) pp. 91–109

Bligh's crew in the open boat were similarly short of rations. They had all made an agreement at the outset to abide by the meagre portions that were necessary if their supplies were to last them long enough to reach land. Some time into the voyage, however, two of the crew noticed that Bligh, when he divided up the rations, kept extra for himself.

As Shackleton and his crew attempt to cross the open sea to Elephant Island in their little boats, he realises that the ocean's swell is moving them further away from their goal. He doesn't tell the whole truth to the crew, however, but simply says that progress is slower than they had hoped. And later, on reaching land, he allows the men to enjoy this achievement and get some rest before letting them know just how dangerous their situation still is.

When Bligh and his men made landfall on an uninhabited island to search for food, he was impatient to set off again. He wanted to reach civilisation so that he could report the mutineers of the *Bounty* who had set them adrift. The crew wanted more time on land, to rest and find food. Bligh flew into a temper and screamed at them. They should be grateful to him, he screamed, because it's only his navigation skills that would get them to safety.

When the crew's carpenter challenges Shackleton's leadership, Shackleton tells him he will not allow one person's lack of cooperation to put the future of the rest in danger.

When Bligh's carpenter made a similar challenge, Bligh attempted to fight it out with swords.

When the cook falls ill, Shackleton gives the task of cooking to one of the crew who seemed to have given up all hope and wanted only to lie down and die. He says:

> *The task of keeping the galley fire alight was both difficult and strenuous, and it took his thoughts away from the chances of immediate dissolution.*
>
> Shackleton (1999) p. 162

Bligh's crew, on the other hand, was made to feel useless. At every turn he reminded them that without him and his navigational skills they would have had no hope of survival.

Bligh drove his crew to press on with their voyage because he was impatient to bring down revenge on the *Bounty* mutineers.

Shackleton drives his crew on because he knows that a sense of purpose and achievement are good for morale: He writes:

> *It will be much better for the men in general to feel that even though progress is slow, they are on their way to land, than it will be simply to sit down and wait for the tardy north-westerly drift to take us out of this cruel waste of ice.*
>
> Shackleton (1999) p. 82

Discussion

So what can we conclude from this about the kind of leadership behaviours that are likely to motivate, and what leadership behaviours would tend to have the opposite effect? Taking the incidents one by one, these are some of the general points we might come up with.

Shackleton begins by praising his crew and expressing his trust in them and in a successful outcome. Bligh, on the other hand, inadvertently fills them with foreboding rather than with hope.

One motivates with praise and trust, the other instils fear about the future.

The way the two leaders utilise food is interesting. Shackleton sees it as a means of raising morale; Bligh sees it as something he must compete with his crew for. If we take food here, in the most basic terms, to be a reward, we see Shackleton using reward to motivate others, while Bligh seems to feel his own entitlement to reward supercedes that of his crew. This raises questions about the uses and abuses of power and about self-interest. It is also significant here that Shackleton sees the rations as a way to inject a small element of surprise and novelty into the daily routine. We might summarise all this thus.

One uses reward (food, novelty) to motivate the crew, while the other focuses on his own rewards.

Here we see something very similar. The issue here, too, is about goals and rewards. It is also about priorities. For Bligh, his own goal (reaching civilization and bringing the mutineers to justice) takes priority over the goals and aspirations of his crew, which are about regaining sufficient health and strength to make the rest of the voyage safely. There is something here, too, about expectations. Bligh expects gratitude and obedience, whereas

Shackleton focuses on what his crew's expectations might be. Bligh also loses his temper – and quite spectacularly, too. This loss of control over his own behaviour is mirrored by his deteriorating control over the behaviour of others. We might summarise all this thus.

One leader focuses on the goals and expectations of his crew, while the other focuses largely on his own;

and

one maintains self-control, while the other doesn't.

CLOSE FOCUS CLOSE FOCUS CLOSE FOCUS CLOSE FOCUS CLOSE FOCUS **CLOSE FOCUS**

Shackleton keeps the whole truth from his crew. He doesn't let them know immediately how perilous their position still is. His reasoning is that they need to keep their spirits up in order to carry on. Is this justified, do you think? Translating this into classroom terms, would you ever feel it was justified to mislead learners about, for example, the quality of their performance or the chances of their success, if by misleading them you might raise their performance or improve their chances?

In dealing with conflict the two again take very different approaches. Although both confront the troublemaker, Bligh chooses to escalate the situation into a fight. He adopts a position in which it is him alone in opposition to the crew. Shackleton, on the other hand, draws the lines very differently. He turns the situation into one in which it is he who is protecting the interests of the rest of the crew against the troublemaker.

The one leader adopts a 'me against them' position which escalates the confrontation, while the other adopts an 'us against him' position which defuses the situation.

Shackleton raises morale by making individuals feel useful. Bligh makes his crew feel useless by constantly reminding them that they are entirely dependent upon him to navigate them to safety. In this way he undermines morale.

One motivates by building others' self-esteem, and one demotivates by undermining it.

Intent upon his own goal and his own agenda, Bligh demonstrates no ability to imagine how the crew might be feeling nor to take this into consideration. Shackleton, however, shows himself acutely aware of his crew's state of mind, and uses this awareness to inform his decision-making.

One behaves towards his crew with empathy; the other does not.

And so we now have the basis for describing two opposing styles of leadership behaviour. Let's move away from crews and ice and open boats, and let's talk about learners and colleges and classrooms. In the context of teaching and learning we might call these two styles the Shackleton model and the Bligh model of motivation and classroom management. Set out side by side, they would look something like this.

Shackleton model	Bligh model
Motivates with praise and trust	Instils fear for the future
Rewards learners to motivate them	Looks only for own reward
Focuses on the goals and expectations of learners	Focuses on own goals
Manages own behaviour effectively	Loses self-control e.g. loses temper
Builds up learners' self-esteem	Undermines learners' self-esteem
Behaves towards learners with empathy	Behaves insensitively towards learners

How would you describe the difference between the attitude of each of these two leaders towards those in their charge?

With these two models of classroom management now clearly set out we can more easily see what it is about the attitudes of the two leaders which made them have such different effects on their crew. Shackleton's actions and decisions seem to be motivated by his care for others. Bligh's, on the other hand, don't appear to take others into account much at all. Shackleton is concerned not only with the physical welfare of his men, but also for their state of mind. Bligh doesn't seem able or willing to take others' feelings into account. Now of course we may be doing Captain Bligh a grave disservice here. For all we know he may have been a perfectly pleasant and sensitive sort of bloke, who just couldn't cope with other people's feelings. History is notoriously unreliable on these matters. But it's handy for our present purposes – and more fun – if we take history at face value and continue to use him as our model of what not to do.

The Shackleton model of motivation and classroom management, as we've set it out here, could be said to be based upon what Goleman (1996) calls 'emotional intelligence'. Emotional intelligence, put very simply, is not only an awareness of your own feelings and motivation, but also an ability to take others' feelings and sensitivities into account, or to be able to imagine yourself in someone else's shoes. If we can do this – if we can imagine what our learners may be feeling, if we can see things for a moment from their point of view – we can use this to inform our interactions with them. If we take the time to realise, for example, that they might be feeling unequal to the demands of the course, we may well put a very different interpretation on their failure to hand work in on time, or on their persistent time-wasting in class. We can see Shackleton using his emotional intelligence all the time. This man is losing heart – give him a task that concentrates his mind; these are afraid their efforts will fail – remind them of their strengths and make them feel good about themselves. And we can also see quite clearly how Bligh fails altogether to do this. He tells scary stories of cannibalism to men cast adrift in an open boat; he loses his temper and picks fights with men who are dependent upon him for reaching safety. How sensitive – how emotionally intelligent – is that? If we can take a moment to imagine ourselves in our learners' shoes we are likely to gain a much clearer idea of how best to motivate them and gain their co-operation.

Celebrating success

Looking at explorers stranded on the ice and castaways lost at sea may seem a strange way to approach issues about classroom practice. But these are people who are in danger of losing their hope; and we have seen already how loss of hope may be an important factor in some of our learners' reluctance to engage with learning. One of the ways we can motivate those who feel they have little to hope for from education and training is to find successes – however minor – to celebrate. This is another difference between the Shackleton model and Bligh model: Shackleton finds things to praise and celebrate – the men's courage, for example, or a tiny variation in diet – while Bligh finds things to criticise and feel fearful of. The Shackleton model of motivation and classroom management involves, among other things, putting the flags out. This doesn't mean giving undeserved praise. Sometimes criticism is necessary. But we don't have to do it Bligh's way. We can do it the emotionally intelligent way by using what Goleman (1996) refers to as the 'artful critique' (pp. 153–54). This means that the feedback we give focuses on what has been achieved and what *could* be achieved, rather than on what has not been achieved. In this way we are able to give some credit for any effort made, and any achievement, however small, and we are able at the same time to describe clearly what still needs to be done. Good teachers have been doing this for a long time. The name we would give it would be 'accurate, helpful and constructive feedback'.

So what links can we make here to classroom practice?

You'll probably have come up with some examples here of your own experience, as a teacher, or as a colleague observing someone else's class, or as a learner yourself, when you have seen one or other of these models in practice. Let's have a bit of fun now, and look at how a modern proponent of the Bligh model might go about tackling the problem of unmotivated learners. We'll call her Billie Bligh and we'll see how she handles a situation in which Jewell, a learner, has repeatedly failed to hand in any coursework.

CLOSE FOCUS CLOSE FOCUS CLOSE FOCUS CLOSE FOCUS CLOSE FOCUS **CLOSE FOCUS**

See if you can identify the key characteristics of the Bligh model at work here.

Billie: *OK. That's it. You can all clear off. Not you, Jewell. You come here. I want a word with you.*

Jewell: *What?*

Billie: *Where's your assignment?*

Jewell: *I haven't got it. I've got to go—*

Billie: *You leave this room before I've finished what I've got to say to you and there's going to be trouble.*

Jewell: *What? You can't do nothing to me.*

Billie: *That's what you think, is it?*

Jewell: *Go on, then. What can you do to me?*

Billie: *Where's your assignment?*

Jewell: *I've told you. I haven't done it.*

Billie: *You haven't done it. Why haven't you done it?*

Jewell: *Because it's boring.*

Billie: *Not as boring as being on the dole all your life. Is that what you want? Is that what you're after? Because that's what you're heading for. Never affording a decent place to live, or a car, or a holiday, or any of that. Just daytime TV and—*

▶

> Jewell: *Well that's good, then, innit, because I like daytime TV.*
>
> Billie: *Well that doesn't surprise me a bit. And it's a good thing you do. Because if you're not going to do any work you're going to fail this course and you're not going to get a job and you're going to spend all your miserable life watching daytime TV.*
>
> Jewell: *Ah, piss off.*
>
> Billie: *What did you say?*
>
> Jewell: *I'm going.*
>
> Billie: *Come here!*
>
> Jewell: *I said I'm going. What you going to do about it?*
>
> Billie: *I'll tell you what I'm going to do about it—*
>
> (But Jewell has gone.)

Discussion

Well, all the Bligh ingredients are there, aren't they? Billie handles this:

✗ in a manner likely to escalate the conflict: 'That's what you think, is it?';

✗ aggressively: 'all your miserable life';

✗ confrontationally: 'You come here. I want a word with you';

✗ using fear as a motivator: 'and there's going to be trouble';

✗ by undermining self-esteem: 'being on the dole all your life';

✗ using criticism but no praise: 'Well that doesn't surprise me a bit'.

We'll have a look now at how Tina Shackleton would handle the same situation, using – naturally – the Shackleton model of management and motivation.

CLOSE FOCUS CLOSE FOCUS CLOSE FOCUS CLOSE FOCUS CLOSE FOCUS **CLOSE FOCUS**

Again, see if you can identify the key characteristics of this model at work.

> Tina: *Alright. Now, before you go – Listen a minute! – Before you go I just need to see one or two people for a quick word. Jewell, I'd like to see you first, now please. Don't worry, you won't miss your break. It'll only take a couple of minutes.*
>
> Jewell: *What?*
>
> Tina: *It's OK. I just need to talk to you about your assignment.*
>
> Jewell: *I haven't done it, if that's what you're on about.*
>
> Tina: *OK. Do you want to tell me why?*
>
> Jewell: *No. Can I go?*

Tina: *Seriously, Jewell. I'd like to know.*

Jewell: *No point, is there?*

Tina: *Why do you say that?*

Jewell: *There isn't, is there. What's the point?*

Tina: *I don't know. I just think you'd be able to make a really good job of it if you gave it a try.*

Jewell: *Me? No way!*

Tina: *I think you're too modest.*

Jewell: *(Laughs) Oh yeah!*

Tina: *Yeah. I reckon you could do it. I bet you'd have some interesting things to say as well.*

Jewell: *If you could read it.*

Tina: *You'd be surprised what I can read. Unusual spelling, unusual handwriting. I've seen it all. Anyway, if you do it on the computer you can put the spellcheck on it. Email it to me and I can put the spellcheck on it.*

Jewell: *Teachers aren't supposed to need a spellcheck.*

Tina: *Don't you believe it. You going to do it for me then?*

Jewell: *Maybe.*

Tina: *Go on, then, or you'll miss your break.*

Discussion

This certainly looks more hopeful. One of the things we notice immediately is that Tina stops when she's winning. She gets a 'maybe' out of Jewell, and she doesn't press it any further. She clearly judges that she's made enough headway for now. Next time they talk about it she'll be starting from a much better position. Knowing when to stop is a good example of the use of emotional intelligence. Press it any further at this point and she could lose him. As it stands, she has managed in this interaction to communicate the following things to Jewell:

✓ She cares about his well-being: 'Go on, then, or you'll miss your break';

✓ She is interested in him: 'I bet you'd have some interesting things to say';

✓ She values what he has to say: 'Seriously, Jewell. I'd like to know';

✓ She believes he is capable of meeting the demands of the course: 'I just think you'd be able to make a really good job of it';

✓ She won't be judgemental about his spelling or writing: 'Unusual spelling, unusual handwriting. I've seen it all';

✓ She has a good opinion of him: 'I think you're too modest';

✓ She is reasonable: 'Don't worry, you won't miss your break';

✓ She has a sense of humour: 'Don't you believe it'.

This is quite a lot to achieve in the space of one short dialogue, and Tina makes it look simple. But when we remind ourselves of the way Billie handles the same situation, we see how easy it would be to get it completely wrong.

Tina does some interesting things here. She defuses the potential confrontation by side-stepping the learner's belligerence:

Jewell: *'I haven't done it, if that's what you're on about'*;

Tina: *'OK. Do you want to tell me why?'*;

Jewell: *'No. Can I go?'*;

Tina: *'Seriously, Jewell. I'd like to know'*.

At the same time she is making the point that she cares. And she responds in an interesting way to the 'no point' argument. She doesn't try to persuade him that there is a point – in the sense that he intends – but instead she provides him with an alternative point, and that is that she would be interested in what he has to say. Instead of contradicting him, therefore, and possibly adding to his sense of grievance and inadequacy, she uses his negative, pessimistic comment 'What's the point?' as an opportunity to boost the learner's self-esteem. We can also see her testing out an intuition that one of the reasons Jewell hasn't handed work in might be a self-consciousness about spelling or presentation. The way she approaches this shows a high degree of emotional intelligence. She refers to 'unusual' spelling. She makes no value judgement about it; and she also treats it humorously. In this way she raises the issue and at the same time defuses it, so that the learner will be clear that there is nothing to fear here.

If we had to sum up here the difference between these two approaches – the difference between Billie and Tina – we could say that Billie makes the learner feel unvalued and afraid for the future, while Tina makes him feel valued and optimistic. It's Tina who puts the flags out.

Other attributes

Following this dialogue on the page, however, we won't see what is perhaps one of the most important aspects of teacher–learner interaction. It is, of course, not only what you say, but how you say it that counts. We might call this managing by example. We began to get a glimpse of how this works in Chapter 6 when we followed Gloria into her two alternative futures. It works in two ways. Firstly, if we look again at the way Tina and Billie behave during the interaction, we can see that Tina – like Gloria in the first of her alternative scenarios – models the behaviour that she would wish the learner to adopt. She is reasonable; she doesn't lose her temper; she sidesteps conflict and aggression; she uses her sense of humour; she behaves towards the learner with respect; and she adopts an open, friendly manner. Now, if this is the way she wishes the learner to act, what better method than demonstrating it for the learner by her own behaviour? Billie, on the other hand, provides a rather unfortunate model of behaviour: aggressive, confrontational, and generally negative. Her method for encouraging appropriate behaviour would clearly be not 'do what I do', but only 'do what I say'.

The other aspect of interaction which it's impossible to replicate on the page is body language. And here, again, the same principle of modelling can apply. It is well-known among those who advise on interview techniques that any face-to-face interaction involves a certain amount of 'mirroring'; that is to say that one participant in an interaction may be affected by, and begin to mirror, the body language of another. If, for example, Tina adopts a relaxed, friendly body language – smiling, nodding, arms uncrossed – there is a good chance that these signals will, even if he's not consciously aware of it, make Jewell feel more relaxed and accepted and at ease, and, what is more, he himself will begin to mirror them. You can test this for yourself the next time an appropriate situation arises. Try nodding, almost imperceptibly, as you are talking to someone; and the chances are you'll find them mirroring this body language back to you – a very positive and affirmative thing to have happening in any meeting! On the other hand, if Billie folds her arms, or wags a finger, or scowls, the learner is likely to mirror exactly that negative or aggressive body language back at her, thus escalating the sense of confrontation.

Conclusion

We have looked here at two opposing styles of classroom leadership, and illustrated how one is more effective in motivating learners and managing difficult behaviour. We have also seen how the teacher can themselves provide a model of appropriate behaviour, and can use positive body language to improve teacher–learner communication. What this chapter illustrates, too, I hope, is that we can learn some useful things about leadership and motivation without having to go to academic texts on the subject. We can encounter examples and ideas on which to reflect in the ordinary course of reading for pleasure, or watching television, or simply by keeping an eye open for what's going on around us.

A SUMMARY OF KEY POINTS A SUMMARY OF KEY POINTS A SUMMARY OF KEY POINTS

In this chapter we have:

> **identified some of the qualities and strategies that enable a leader to motivate others and secure their cooperation;**

> **considered ways in which we can apply some of these to our own practice in the classroom or workshop;**

> **identified some of the attitudes and behaviours which the teacher should avoid as being counter-productive to encouraging positive behaviour and motivation in learners;**

> **explored two models of behaviour management: one positive and the other negative;**

> **considered the importance of emotional intelligence and accurate, helpful and constructive feedback in motivating learners and helping them to manage their behaviour;**

> **looked at how body language may affect teacher-learner interactions.**

Branching options

The following three options are designed to provide you with additional opportunities for reflection, analysis and research. You may choose the option which best supports your currently identified needs, as set out, for example, in your action plan for a teaching qualification or for your continuing professional development (CPD). Alternatively, you may choose to work through two or even all three tasks.

1. *Reflection*
   - Take some time to reflect on your teaching over the past week. What sort of strategies or tactics have you used in your attempts to manage learners' behaviour and to motivate them to engage with their learning? Are you a Shackleton or are you a Bligh? Does your subject influence your approach in any way? If you find, on reflection, that you're a little of each, what practical strategies could you adopt to move further towards the Shackleton model?
   - Remember to evaluate whether or how well these work when you put them into practice.

2. *Analysis*
   - Arrange to have yourself videoed while you are teaching and then analyse the recording, carefully taking note of the body language you are using. Or, if the very thought of that horrifies you, arrange instead for a colleague or mentor to observe you teaching and then to give you feedback on your body language.
   - Did anything you saw or were told surprise you? What sort of attitude/s towards your learners did your body language convey? How enthusiastic did you appear about your specialist subject? Did your body language change when you were addressing issues of learner behaviour? What did it convey?
   - Reflect on what you have learnt from this exercise, and what changes it might cause you to introduce into your future practice.

3. *Research*
   - Use the internet or library facilities to find out more about emotional intelligence and the theory of multiple intelligences.
   - In what ways can you apply what you've learnt from this research to your own practice in teaching your subject and in motivating learners and managing their behaviour?

REFERENCES AND FURTHER READING REFERENCES AND FURTHER READING

Goleman, D. (1996) *Emotional Intelligence*. London: Bloomsbury.

If you'd like to read more about Shackleton or Bligh, and their styles of leadership, some interesting books include:

Kennedy, G. (1989) *Captain Bligh: The Man and his Mutinies*. London: Duckworth Press.
Lansing, A. (1994) *Endurance: Shackleton's Incredible Voyage*. NY: Carroll and Graf.
Morrell, M. and Capparell, S. (2001) *Shackleton's Way*. London: Nicholas Brealey.
Shackleton, E. (1999) *South: Journals of his Last Expedition to Antarctica*. London: Robson.
Toohey, J. (1998) *Captain Bligh's Portable Nightmare*. London: Fourth Estate.

11
Teachers talking

A teacher affects eternity; he can never tell where his influence stops.
Henry Adams, 1907

The objectives of this chapter

This chapter relates, in teachers' own words, some of the most difficult or confrontational incidents they have had to deal with. It analyses and evaluates the strategies they have used, and invites you to do the same. The purpose of the chapter is to present you with a range of possible solutions to difficult situations.

Introduction

The material in this chapter is based upon responses from 100 teachers working in the FE sector. One of the questions they were asked was: To what extent have you observed or encountered learner behaviour in the classroom or workshop which has had a negative effect on other learners' opportunity to learn? Over half the teachers replied that they encountered this often or even every day. Not one teacher was able to claim that they had never encountered such behaviour. It is important, therefore, to bear in mind, particularly if you are a new or inexperienced teacher, that it is not unusual to encounter disruptive learner behaviour; nor is it a sign of failure on your part. All FE teachers will encounter it at some time or another; many will encounter it regularly. The professional issue for us as teachers is not whether it happens, but how to deal with it when it does, and how to minimise the likelihood of it happening again.

How do we define disruptive behaviour?

You'll notice that the question was about 'behaviour which has a negative effect on other learners' ability to learn'. This is because if we asked a question about 'disruptive' behaviour, we would run into difficulties. 'Disruptive behaviour' could be interpreted in different ways. We all have different levels of tolerance. What you find disruptive, I might find simply a little lively. An illustration of this is the response of one teacher who, asked to give an example of behaviour which disrupted learning, responded with: 'Excessive talking and general disruption *but nothing of magnitude*' (my italics). Some of us might suggest that excessive talking and general disruption was of magnitude enough!

But by focusing on learning, we go straight to the heart of the issue. Unacceptable or inappropriate behaviour should not be defined according to whether you or I approve of it, or can tolerate it, but by whether it presents a barrier to others' learning. Our role as teachers is to support learning. *Anything which undermines learning becomes a problem which we, as professionals, need to address*.

The most commonly cited examples of behaviour which disrupts learning were the following.

- Talking while the teacher talks and/or talking about things irrelevant to the lesson.
- Arriving late.
- Using or answering mobile phones.
- Distracting other learners' attention.
- Complaining and refusing to work.
- Expressing boredom and lack of interest.

For some teachers, it seems, these kinds of behaviours have become such a normal part of their classroom experience that they take them for granted and simply try to work around them. But if they were to look at this behaviour through a different perspective – the eyes of a newcomer to the profession, for example – they would have to acknowledge that there's a sign here that all is not well. One new recruit to teaching in FE who had been observing some more experienced colleagues reports that:

> *During my first week I observed teachers allowing learners to come and go as they pleased, talk while they were talking and eat packets of crisps etc. throughout the lesson.*

Another confides:

> *There certainly seems to be a leniency beyond any experience I have encountered.*

A question they both go on to reflect upon is: Why are the learners there at all if their intention is not to learn and, in the process, to disrupt the learning of others? In Chapter 2 we looked at some possible answers to this question; in this chapter we shall take a pragmatic approach and consider some strategies for dealing with such situations on a day-to-day basis. It is important to remember, however, that the underlying reasons for learners behaving in this way may often originate with policies which are drawn up and implemented at a national, regional or institutional level. What we can do at the classroom level is to deal with immediate and specific situations. We can't affect trends of attitude and behaviour; only the policy-makers can do that. One teacher described this as 'Holding the fort from day to day while we wait for the cavalry to arrive and bring better times.' This may be how it feels sometimes; but there is nevertheless a professional satisfaction to be gained when we succeed in supporting learning in the face of difficult circumstances.

TASK TASK TASK **TASK** TASK TASK **TASK** TASK TASK **TASK** TASK TASK

Let's go back to those recurrent disruptive behaviours listed above. What would you say they have in common? You may like to jot down a few notes before continuing to read.

Discussion

Well, clearly the first thing they have in common is that, although they present difficulties for those learners in the class who may want to learn, they are not in themselves, taken singly, particularly serious breaches of manners or of discipline. (Don't worry. We'll be coming to some of those later!) They are non-violent and non-confrontational. They all indicate a lack of commitment and lack of interest rather than a serious intention to cause trouble. They seem to indicate one of two things: either that the learner is bored and unmotivated, or that they are hoping to avoid having to do work that may stretch them beyond what they consider to be their abilities. Looked at in this way, the behaviour presents problems which may be open to a number of solutions.

Common behaviour management strategies

Let's have a look now at some of the strategies our sample of teachers used. Here's a list of some of the ways teachers addressed the most commonly encountered disruption – learners talking while the teacher is trying to speak to the class.

- Give informal warnings and initiate formal report procedures.
- Ignore it. I'm not empowered to rectify this.
- Plan more group-work, so that they get a chance to talk, and I get a chance to focus what they talk about.
- Allocate ten minutes at the start of each lesson to have a chat (informally chaired by me) which allows them to catch up on one another's news, TV programmes watched, etc. Then we get down to work.
- Frighten them by reminding them they've got unit tests to do.
- Ask them to stop talking.
- Reassure them by saying the lesson's nearly over and they'll be able to talk about whatever they like to whoever they like afterwards.
- Ask them what the problem was.
- Just keep telling them to quieten down and get on with their work.
- Move the noisiest learner as far away as possible from the rest, right at the front where I can see him.
- Stop talking and stare at the learners involved. The others then tell them to shut up.
- Tell them they can't go for break until they've shut up and listened.
- Tackle them, loudly and aggressively. Make them jump.
- Just talk more loudly so the rest can hear me.
- Direct some of my questions at the noisy ones to try to draw them in.
- Report them to their personal tutor.
- Draw up some individual, achievable goals with them.
- Warn them and, if they persist, tell them to get out.
- Break the next session up: input, then learner activity; input, then learner activity. That way they don't have to listen for too long, and they have something to get actively involved in.
- Speak to those concerned separately and remind them of the ground-rules.
- Set a target for that learner to achieve in that lesson.

TASK TASK TASK **TASK** TASK TASK **TASK** TASK TASK **TASK** TASK TASK

How would you evaluate each of these strategies? How would you estimate their chances of success? You may wish to discuss this with a colleague or a mentor, or you may find it useful as a starting point for a reflective entry in your journal.

Discussion

As that long list suggests, there are certainly plenty of strategies to try, and what works in one situation will not necessarily work in another. But in the process of evaluating these responses it is likely that you have come to some conclusions about the *kinds* of strategies that are most likely to be effective, and those which stand least chance of succeeding.

You may have noticed that the strategies listed there fall into two broad categories: those where the teacher *reacts* by trying to *impose* order – for example, 'Warn them, and if they persist, tell them to get out'; or 'Just talk more loudly so the rest can hear me'; and those where the teacher becomes *proactive* and takes steps to *create* order – for example, 'Plan more group-work, so that they get a chance to talk, and I get a chance to focus what they talk about'; or 'Allocate ten minutes at the start of each lesson to have a chat (informally chaired by me) which allows them to catch up on one another's news, TV programmes watched, etc. Then we get down to work'. One of the characteristics which distinguishes between these two is that the proactive, creative approach will normally involve some element of planning; while the reactive attempt to impose order is, as the word 'reactive' suggests, an immediate and perhaps unconsidered response to the unwanted behaviour. Another way to view this would be that the proactive, planned response is more likely to be the outcome of careful reflection on previous practice or observation, whilst the reactive approach may have involved no reflection at all.

CLOSE FOCUS CLOSE FOCUS CLOSE FOCUS CLOSE FOCUS CLOSE FOCUS **CLOSE FOCUS**

1. **You may like to take some time to divide the list into two sub-groups: imposing order and creating order (you can compare your version with the lists at the end of this section).**

2. **In the process of doing this, did you identify any strategies which don't fit clearly into either sub-group?**

Let's take just one of those strategies now and look at it in more detail.

Move the noisiest learner as far away as possible from the rest, right at the front where I can see him.

Essentially, this is a reactive attempt to impose order. We probably all recognise it. It is a measure quite often resorted to, and seems, on the face of it, to make perfect sense. It has, however, one serious flaw, which is this: if you move a noisy or attention-seeking learner to the front of the classroom or workshop, you provide them with the perfect vantage point from which to continue 'entertaining' the rest of the class. They have only to turn in their seat, and they can meet the eyes of their entire audience. This is the worst possible place to position a disruptive learner. It gives them the floor. It makes them a more effective rival for the class's attention. Certainly, they are now within your reach. But to what purpose? You can hardly use force to make them work; and although you may be able to see clearly whether they are on task or not, this is still not a strategy for supporting their learning. At least if you seat them at the back of the room, or the lab or workshop where it is not easy for the other learners to see them and to have their attention distracted, the majority will be able to get on with their work, and the talkative learner *may* fall relatively silent for want of an audience and get on with some work themselves.

Going back to our list of strategies, this is how I would subdivide them.

Imposing order

- Give informal warnings and initiate formal report procedures.
- Ask them to stop talking.
- Frighten them by reminding them they've got unit tests to do.
- Just keep telling them to quieten down and get on with their work.
- Move the noisiest learner as far away as possible from the rest, right at the front where I can see him.
- Tell them they can't go for break until they've shut up and listened.

- Tackle them, loudly and aggressively. Make them jump.
- Just talk more loudly so the rest can hear me.
- Report them to their personal tutor.
- Warn them, and if they persist, tell them to get out.

Creating order

- Plan more group-work, so that they get a chance to talk, and I get a chance to focus what they talk about.
- Allocate ten minutes at the start of each lesson to have a chat (informally chaired by me) which allows them to catch up on one another's news, TV programmes watched, etc. Then we get down to work.
- Draw up some individual, achievable goals with them.
- Break the next session up: input, then learner activity; input, then learner activity. That way they don't have to listen for too long, and they have something to get actively involved in.
- Speak to those concerned separately and remind them of the ground-rules.
- Set a target for that learner to achieve in that lesson.

TASK TASK TASK **TASK** TASK TASK **TASK** TASK TASK **TASK** TASK TASK

Which of these two groups of strategies do you think would be more effective in the long term, and why?

Discussion

I've left out the ones which I don't think sit neatly in either category. Let's just have a look at each of these briefly.

> *Ignore it. I'm not empowered to rectify this.*

This presents like a strategy, but I would argue that it is simply avoidance or denial. As professional practitioners our business is to support learning. If disruptive talk is preventing learning, then what are we achieving by being in the classroom and doing nothing about it? We may as well present our lesson to an empty room. We may not be 'empowered to rectify' learners' disaffection in general, but we have undertaken to do our best to support these particular students' learning. Our professional values dictate that we should at least reflect on how best to do this.

> *Reassure them by saying the lesson's nearly over and they'll be able to talk about whatever they like to whoever they like afterwards.*

Reassure them that the lesson's nearly over? They're not serving a custodial sentence. They're not at the dentist. If they need that sort of reassurance, perhaps the teacher would do better to reflect on how to plan a lesson that would make such reassurances unnecessary.

> *Direct some of my questions at the noisy ones to try to draw them in.*

This strikes me as quite a good strategy. In that respect it is an exception to the 'Imposing order' list. It is a strategy which suggests some reflection.

Stop talking and stare at the learners involved. The others then tell them to shut up.

The same applies to this. Of course, it depends on whether you can cultivate 'the look'! But the use of peer pressure to establish relative quiet will usually be more effective than the teacher trying to impose it on their own; and it steps outside the unproductive Teacher *v.* Learners construct that we have already explored in earlier chapters.

More behaviour management strategies

We began by looking at some of the most commonly cited examples of disruptive behaviour. We'll go on now to look at some of the other kinds of challenging or confrontational situations described by our group of 100 teachers; and we'll consider the strategies, both general and specific, which they used to deal with them.

TASK TASK TASK **TASK** TASK TASK **TASK** TASK TASK **TASK** TASK TASK

Read through the list below, and reflect on how you yourself might deal with each situation. Think this through carefully before proceeding to the next section where we find out what action was actually taken by the teachers concerned. You may like to note down your ideas in your reflective journal and then evaluate them against what these teachers have to say.

- Constant shouting across the classroom.

- Turning on the gas taps in the laboratory.

- Sporadic attendance and failure to hand in work.

- Verbal abuse – being rude to the teacher.

- A learner started taking his clothes off.

- Listening to music on their iPod when they should be listening to the teacher or getting on with work.

- Using tools in the workshop to fight with.

- Arguing with the teacher.

- Running about the room – won't stay in their seats.

No. I'm pleased to say that this wasn't all happening in the same class. These behaviours are not quite so frequently reported as those in our first list; but most of these, I would suggest, are more difficult to deal with and are potentially more serious. We'll take them one by one, consider the teacher's response, and decide whether this was the best (or only) way of dealing with the situation.

Discussion

Constant shouting across the classroom.

Here's the strategy the teacher used:

I tried telling them to be quiet. I tried several times, but it had no effect. In the end I sat them all together, the ones who'd been shouting at each other. My thinking was: if they're going to talk to each other anyway I might as well make it possible for them to do it without disrupting the rest of the class. That particular crowd – four of them – didn't get anything done. But at least the rest of the learners could hear themselves think now, and they got quite a lot done.

This is a very pragmatic approach. It seems to be based on some degree of reflection, and what it amounts to is a strategy of damage limitation – accepting that the four noisy ones won't work anyway, and giving up on them for the sake of the rest.

CLOSE FOCUS CLOSE FOCUS CLOSE FOCUS CLOSE FOCUS CLOSE FOCUS **CLOSE FOCUS**

PROFESSIONAL VALUES

Are there occasions, in your view, on which it is justified to give up on the minority in order to support the learning of the majority?

Turning the gas taps on in the laboratory.

Here's the strategy the teacher used.

I stopped the class. I sent one of the more sensible learners to fetch the Section Head of Science from her office. I told her what had happened and I asked her to remove the learners concerned. She did so. I then explained to the rest of the class the possible consequences of such irresponsible behaviour. Then we resumed the practical session.

The learners' behaviour was not simply disruptive; it was extremely dangerous. The teacher was right to treat the incident very seriously. He was right to stop the class. He was right to have the learners removed. Will they be allowed back in? Will he have to go through all this again? We just don't know. Certainly he was lucky in having his Section Head within summoning distance, and fortunate, too, that she removed the offending learners. Not every teacher has this option under such circumstances. Did you notice how he used the incident as an opportunity to reinforce for the remaining learners some important rules about Health and Safety?

CLOSE FOCUS CLOSE FOCUS CLOSE FOCUS CLOSE FOCUS CLOSE FOCUS **CLOSE FOCUS**

PROFESSIONAL VALUES

If the Section Head had not been willing or available to offer support, what would have been this teacher's best alternative course of action?

Sporadic attendance and failure to hand in work.

Here's the strategy the teacher used.

I chase them up all the time. I report them to their personal tutor. I email them at their college mailbox. It doesn't seem to make any difference. When they do turn up they're completely behind with everything and I have to go over old stuff with them and the others get bored. It's not fair on the ones who turn up regularly. And if I wasn't chasing assignments from the others, I'd have more time to spend giving feedback to those who do hand work in. It's not one or two. It's about a third of the class.

This teacher is so busy being reactive – chasing the learners – that she probably feels she has no time for reflection. It might, however, be worth her while to get these learners talking (once she does catch them!) in the hopes of discovering whether there is any way she could turn them into more regular attenders. There might be ways in which she could rethink her planning, for example, in order to include a wider range of teaching and learning strategies. On the other hand, this is post-compulsory education. And sporadic attendance and non-completion of coursework is a widespread phenomenon which, as we saw in Chapter 2, may arise from causes other than the teacher's classroom practice. This being the case, any strategy on the part of any one teacher will have a limited effect and will not be likely to address the underlying issues.

CLOSE FOCUS CLOSE FOCUS CLOSE FOCUS CLOSE FOCUS CLOSE FOCUS **CLOSE FOCUS**

PROFESSIONAL VALUES

How much effort should the teacher put in to chasing these learners and their coursework? At what point is she justified in putting the more motivated learners' interests first?

Verbal abuse – being rude to the teacher.

Here's the strategy the teacher used.

Sometimes I think it's ok to act like you haven't heard. Sometimes that's better than making an issue of it. But this time I couldn't really let it go because she used such foul language and it was obvious that everybody had heard. I rounded on her and said, 'What did you say?' With hindsight I can see that was a stupid thing to do, because then she got to say it again, and there were one or two sniggers but most of them looked quite shocked. I told her – and them – very firmly that she had overstepped the mark, that she'd gone beyond the boundary of what I found acceptable in my classroom. I didn't shout. I just said it very seriously into the shocked silence that followed her outburst. And I said I would need to speak to her seriously after the class, but I wasn't going to do it now, because it wouldn't be fair to the others if I let her babyish behaviour hold up the rest of the class. I did speak to her afterwards – though I had to follow her down the corridor to do it – and she hasn't re-offended. That was three weeks ago now.

Two things here. The teacher recognises his mistake in asking the learner to repeat what she said. It's an easy mistake to make, though, and arises out of the initial shock of hearing something unacceptable: '*What* did you say?' However, the rest of his strategy looks sound and seems to have succeeded. You'll notice that, by announcing he'll speak to the learner afterwards, he avoids causing an immediate escalation; and by emphasising the care and responsibility he feels towards the other learners, he avoids the possibility of being typecast in the Teacher *v*. Learners construct.

CLOSE FOCUS CLOSE FOCUS CLOSE FOCUS CLOSE FOCUS CLOSE FOCUS **CLOSE FOCUS**

PROFESSIONAL VALUES

The teacher suggests here that it's sometimes alright to turn a deaf ear to students' abuse and to offensive language. What reasons do you think he would give for this? Do you agree with him on this issue? Where would you draw the line between language you would ignore and language you would feel it necessary to confront and actively discourage?

A learner started taking his clothes off.

Here's the strategy the teacher used.

This was a Basic Skills learner who needed a very high level of learning support. I just don't think he realised it wasn't appropriate. I said to him, 'Don't do that. If you're too warm we'll open a window.' His jumper was already on the floor and he was trying to pull his shirt off over his head. The others in the group had all started giggling. There was no way I was going to get any work out of them until he settled down. He was well and truly stuck because he hadn't undone the buttons. I went over and pulled his shirt back down and drew his attention to [the learning support assistant] who'd just come in with one of the other learners. This took his mind off the undressing game, fortunately.

One thing this teacher demonstrates to us is the importance of context when we are considering strategies to deal with difficult behaviour. In her view, this learner wasn't trying to be difficult. He didn't realise that his behaviour was inappropriate. Nevertheless, he doesn't respond to a direct request to stop. The teacher therefore decides to distract him, to focus on something other than the undesirable behaviour. This is the aspect of her strategy that any of us might find useful in a variety of difficult classroom situations. Change the focus. It often works.

CLOSE FOCUS CLOSE FOCUS CLOSE FOCUS CLOSE FOCUS CLOSE FOCUS **CLOSE FOCUS**

PROFESSIONAL VALUES

If this had been a learner on a Level 3 course, or on an HNC in Engineering, rather than on a Basic Skills with Supported Learning programme, would this behaviour have required a different response from the teacher? If you believe it would, what response would be appropriate, and why?

Listening to music on their iPod when they should be listening to the teacher or getting on with work.

Here's the strategy the teacher used.

This happens all the time. It's that or it's phones. Sending text messages to each other. Anyway, I have these ground-rules about phones. Before we start a session I get them all to put their phones on their table where I can see them, and switch them off. So when I caught a couple of them listening to iPods, I stopped the class, waited until everybody was looking eyes front, and then told them that iPods were in the same category as phones. On the table. A few groans. But they did it. I think they're ok with rules as long as you're up front with them and apply them consistently.

This teacher is quite clear about what's acceptable in his classes and what's not. And he makes sure the learners are, too. You might feel that not all learners would be so co-operative, and you may be right. There are some general pointers, however, that we can usefully take from his strategy. He makes sure that he addresses the whole class when he reviews the rules, and he makes sure the whole class hears him. And he emphasises that these rules are an integral part of his classroom practice; in other words, his response to the iPods doesn't appear simply arbitrary and reactive, but rather as consistent with his expectations about classroom behaviour. This is an important point because it almost certainly has some bearing on the learners' eventual compliance.

CLOSE FOCUS CLOSE FOCUS CLOSE FOCUS CLOSE FOCUS CLOSE FOCUS **CLOSE FOCUS**

PROFESSIONAL VALUES

Some teachers claim that they would have confiscated the iPods until the end of the session. What are your views on this? What is your college's policy? What do you believe would be the advantages and disadvantages of confiscation?

Using tools in the workshop to fight with.

Here's the strategy the teacher used.

> *I sent the rest of the class through out of harm's way to the other workshop where Rizwan was teaching. Then I called the police on my mobile. Then I shouted at the two of them that I'd called the police. Then I called security. By the time security arrived (two of them) one bloke had thrown the chisel down and run off, and the other was busy kicking a piece of machinery. We calmed him down. He went off with security. The police arrived. Statements and all that. They caught up with the other bloke in the end. Needless to say, they were both chucked off the course.*

This is a more serious incident than most of us will ever have to deal with. The teacher's strategy, however, is worth remembering. First he gets the rest of the learners to safety; then he calls for assistance. He does not attempt to intervene physically and stop the fight. And he is quite correct in this, since any injury to either man, following his intervention, could quite possibly – even if unjustly – be blamed on him.

CLOSE FOCUS CLOSE FOCUS CLOSE FOCUS CLOSE FOCUS CLOSE FOCUS **CLOSE FOCUS**

PROFESSIONAL VALUES

This teacher took a number of sensible steps. Is there anything about the order they were taken in which you would want to change?

TASK TASK TASK **TASK** TASK TASK **TASK** TASK **TASK** **TASK** TASK TASK

The final two confrontational behaviours in our list are these:

- **arguing with the teacher;**

- **running about the room – won't stay in their seats.**

How would you deal with each of these? If you have already encountered this sort of behaviour, can you remember how you responded? How effective was your response?

Use your journal to outline a strategy – a contingency plan – for the next time these situations arise in one of your classes. You may find it useful to look back over some of the earlier chapters, particularly Chapters 4 and 5, to remind yourself of how other teachers have dealt with a similar challenge.

Can adult learners be confrontational too?

One of the questions our 100 teachers were asked was about the relationship between learners' age and negative behaviour. It is often assumed that it is only the younger, 16–19 (and now perhaps 14–19), age group which presents a challenge to classroom management in FE. However, one third of the teachers who responded to this question replied that they had experienced or observed difficult or negative behaviour from adult learners (that is, those over 21) as well as from the younger (14–19) age group. Perhaps we should not be surprised by this. The policies and practices which impact on adult learners are much the same as those which affect learners in their teens. And with adult learners, as we saw in Chapter 3, there may be added pressures, of time, of family or financial responsibilities and of anxieties about returning to education or training. Moreover, for the teacher, the idea of issuing rules to an adult learner, or challenging their behaviour or pulling them up on their language or attitude, may somehow be more com-plicated than if the learner was a 16-year-old. Whether this is right or wrong is not at issue here. What is important in our current context is that you may feel as though challenging behaviour from an adult is more difficult to deal with than challenging behaviour from a younger learner, particularly if the adult in question is older than you are.

Our sample teachers were asked to describe how they would respond to the following situation. You are teaching a group of adults on an evening Access course. There are 19 of them, aged between 22 and 60. You call the class to order so that you can introduce the topic for the lesson. All the learners give you their attention, except for one middle-aged man who has a newspaper open and is holding it in front of him, obscuring his face and is still apparently reading it. You say, brightly, 'OK. Are we all ready?'

He still doesn't put his paper down. The other learners are looking from you to him and him to you, and you begin to feel embarrassed. You say, 'Colin? Are you in there? Are you going to join us?'

He just grunts, and rattles the paper, and carries on reading.

What do you do next?

Teachers came up with a variety of responses to this situation. The most entertaining – but one we needn't take too seriously – was, 'Set fire to his newspaper.'

Consider what your response to this situation would be.

What might you say?

What might you do?

For each suggestion you come up with, try to follow it through to its possible repercussions.

How might the learner respond?

How might you make him feel?

What might the other learners be thinking or feeling?

Conclusion

As with most situations in teaching, there is no one correct solution. The important thing is that you are able to recognise, and to avoid, the wrong solutions – the ones which will undermine learner confidence or motivation; the ones which will make matters worse or place you, the teacher, in an impossible predicament. When you choose your path of action you need to be sure that it is not simply reactive, but that it is based on careful reflection and, above all, on a careful consideration of your own professional values.

A SUMMARY OF KEY POINTS A SUMMARY OF KEY POINTS A SUMMARY OF KEY POINTS

In this chapter we have:

> discussed what we mean by 'disruptive' behaviour;

> looked at what teachers in the sector have to say about managing learners' inappropriate or disruptive behaviour;

> considered some of the strategies they have used, and evaluated them in terms of their usefulness for our own practice;

> analysed these strategies and categorised them according to whether they are designed to *impose order* (i.e. are reactive)or to *create order* (i.e. are proactive and reflective);

> explored some of the questions about professional values which these strategies raise.

Branching options

The following three options are designed to provide you with additional opportunities for reflection, analysis and research. You may choose the option which best supports your currently identified needs, as set out, for example, in your action plan for a teaching qualification or for your continuing professional development (CPD). Alternatively, you may choose to work through two or even all three tasks.

1. *Reflection*
   - **Select two of the situations listed under the Task on p. 104, and consider how you yourself would deal with them. What might be your immediate (reactive) response? How might your response differ if you were given the opportunity to reflect and plan ahead?**

- Reflecting back on your recent teaching, would you say that in general you tend to try to *impose* order or to *create* order? Does your subject influence your approach?
- Is there anything about your current behaviour management strategies that you could usefully change?

2. *Analysis*
- We've seen the list of learner behaviour most frequently cited by teachers as presenting problems. How does this compare with your own experience? Think back over your recent experience of teaching and jot down what you perceive to be the five most frequently occurring issues of behaviour management. Are they related in any way to your specialist subject?
- Think through how you could address each of these proactively, by *creating* order.
- Try one or more of these tactics in your next lesson, and then analyse what you have learnt from this exercise, and what changes it might cause you to introduce into your future practice.

3. *Research*
- Use the internet or library facilities to find out more about behaviour management in an educational context.
- In what ways can you apply what you've learnt from this research to your own practice in teaching your subject and in motivating learners and managing their behaviour?

REFERENCES AND FURTHER READING REFERENCES AND FURTHER READING

Wallace, S. (2007) *Getting the Buggers Motivated in FE*. London: Continuum.

Wallace, S. (2011) *Teaching, Tutoring and Training in the Lifelong Learning Sector*, 4th edition. Exeter: Learning Matters.

12
So what's happening in FE? What the research is telling us

Today, in our schools, the manual trades are given little honor.
Matthew Crawford, 2011

The objectives of this chapter

This chapter draws together the main themes and arguments that we've explored so far and looks at how these are reflected in the findings of recent research projects and publications. It will be of particular interest if you are looking for sources to underpin your own writing, particularly of assignments you may be undertaking towards a teaching or CPD qualification. It expands on some of the ideas encountered in Chapter 2 about the underlying causes of learner disengagement and identifies specific sources to enable you to explore these further if and when you wish to. It also picks up again the question of usefulness and purpose in relation to education and training, which was raised in Chapter 7. These theoretical perspectives are presented here as an additional way of understanding some of the scenarios we've previously discussed from a pragmatic and practical point of view; and you may find it useful, when you have finished this chapter, to go back and read some of them again with these theoretical arguments in mind.

Introduction

In Chapter 2 we looked briefly at some of the explanations researchers and others have offered for the negative behaviour sometimes encountered in FE. These explanations or theories fall broadly under four categories, which we can summarise as reasons to do with:

- **socio-economic issues;**
- **learners' perception of commonly held views about the status of FE;**
- **the narrowness of the vocational curriculum in its current format;**
- **learners' sense of having no real choice about their progression at 16.**

We're going to have a more detailed look at each of these, and we're going to discuss some cases and situations to illustrate the ways these issues might present in practice.

How socio-economic issues might affect learner behaviour and motivation

Socio-economic issues, in the context of education and training, largely concern matters such as rates of unemployment; the value of earnings against the cost of living; ideas about social class and its links with child poverty and educational disadvantage; and class-driven inequalities of educational provision and access. For example, research has shown that there are far higher percentages of learners from lower socio-economic backgrounds in FE than there are in school sixth forms and sixth form colleges (Foster, 2005). This points to something which may be to do with achievement or with aspirations and expectations, or even with careers advice and guidance; but which presents, in any case, a clear division along class lines. If we think about this in relation to our learners, we can understand how it might appear to some of them that their background or circumstances have, even by the age of 16, imposed limits on their choices about progression and set them on the FE route with an inevitability that they aren't equipped to challenge in any positive way. The only way they can challenge it is through disruption or disengagement. Research also shows that learners who enter FE from a middle-class background are generally those whose academic achievement has been too low to allow them to enter a school sixth form or a sixth form college (Thompson, 2009). This means that for most of them FE is a second best option, the only one open to them because of their 'failure' to gain adequate grades in Year 11. Again, their choice has been constrained and this may understandably lead to resentment and negative behaviour. Taken together, what both these pieces of research suggest is that the idea of FE as a second best route is being perpetuated both by its association with lower social class and with low educational achievement. This affects its public image, an image which learners will be well aware of. Some may, therefore, express any frustrations they feel by acting out what this means for them.

Learners' perception of commonly held views about the status of FE

We've seen how stereotypical ideas about FE and FE learners may be perpetuated through associations with social class and low achievement. Let's pick up now on how this may affect learners' own self-image and the knock-on effect on attitude and behaviour. We looked briefly in Chapter 2 at this question of how the status of vocational education in general – and of FE in particular – may impact on learners' self-esteem. In 2002, Alison Wolf was describing the sector ironically as a provision *for other people's children* (Wolf, 2002, p.56), but not a route we would advise our own to take. Researchers, Swift and Fisher (2012), pick up this point about *the ambivalent status surrounding vocational education* (p. 207) and argue that it is probably this idea of it being somehow second rate which discourages the most able and ambitious students from taking the FE option. Moreover, they also suggest that these notions about its status may contribute to lowering levels of motivation and engagement of some learners who find themselves in FE for want of an alternative. Research also suggests that learners in FE express lower aspirations than those who stay on to study in school sixth forms (Baird et al., 2012). These factors all help to explain why FE is commonly perceived as a route for learners who have 'failed' at school (Thompson, 2009). What all these researchers are helping us to understand is why some of our learners may have been led to feel that making the effort to succeed in FE is simply not worth it.

Ellen-Mae goes to college

Let's have a look now at how these issues about status and class might present themselves in real terms in the circumstances of one typical FE learner. Ellen-Mae is 17 years old and is in her first term at college on a Level 2 Performing Arts course. Her teachers have noticed that she is failing to complete any coursework; she arrives late for practical sessions; she is reluctant to engage in any activity, particularly dance; and that she distracts other learners from their tasks by talking and joking with them. Following a section meeting at which these concerns are raised, the course leader decides to have a word with her to try to find out what her problem is.

TASK TASK **TASK** TASK **TASK** TASK **TASK** TASK **TASK** **TASK** TASK TASK

As you read through the conversation between Ellen-Mae and the course leader, see if you can identify:

- **what's causing this learner to behave in the way she does;**

- **how the research findings we've just considered can contribute to our understanding of her situation;**

- **what her teachers might be able to do to help her.**

CL: *Ellen, come and sit down here with me for a minute, please. I need to talk to you.*

E-M: *It's Ellen-Mae.*

CL: *Sorry. Ellen-Mae. Sit down then, please. Thank you. Now, tell me how you're getting on with the course so far?*

E-M: *It's rubbish.*

CL: *Oh. Well, I'm sorry to hear that you feel like that about it. What is it in particular you don't like?*

E-M: *I don't like any of it. It's stupid. I never wanted to do it in the first place, did I?*

CL: *What did you want to do?*

E-M: *I wanted to do A levels. I wanted to stay at school. The whole point was I wanted to go to university to do Drama. I was going to do English, French and Drama for A level and then go to university. But then I did rubbish in my Year 11 and suddenly the school won't let me go into the sixth form.*

CL: *But you can still go to university. If you do well on this course you can go on to Level 3 and then apply to university that way. FE can give you a route into higher education, just like the sixth form can...*

E-M: *This isn't the same. Performing Arts isn't the same as Drama. I'm supposed to dance and that. I hate dancing. We don't read plays. I want to read plays.*

CL: *So why did you choose this course?*

E-M: *I didn't! I didn't choose it! I couldn't do A levels. The Head of Sixth Form said I should come and do this if I was interested in drama. You know: Go away. We don't want you. Go and do that instead. He obviously didn't know what he was talking about. Both my brothers went to university. Now my mum and dad think I'm some sort of loser because I'm in FE. They don't like telling their friends what I'm doing. They all think FE is for losers...*

CL: *But you know that's not true. You've met people here who are bright like you – interesting, ambitious. You know your parents' image of FE is wrong.*

E-M: *But that doesn't make any difference, does it? As long as people think we're all thick or something.*

CL: *Well, how about we prove them wrong?*

E-M: *Can't be bothered. What's the point?*

Discussion

First of all, how well do you think the course leader handled this conversation? I think she made a pretty good job of it, even though she doesn't arrive at any solution. She asks the right questions. She listens carefully to what this learner has to say. She is non-judgemental in her responses. She tries to build the learner's confidence, reminding her that she's 'bright, interesting and ambitious'. By the end of this conversation – or at least the bit of it that we see here – she has a clear understanding of how Ellen-Mae feels and why, so that she now has an explanation for the negative behaviour that her teachers have reported.

Indeed, this was our first question: *What's causing this learner to behave in the way she does?* The answer is clearly that Ellen-Mae is not on her course by choice. She wanted to stay on at school, but the school wouldn't accept her into the sixth form because of her poor results at the end of Year 11. She has had poor advice from her school where Performing Arts has been confused with Drama. She is from a family in which progression to university seems to be considered the norm and in which FE is associated with failure. Consequently, she regards her place on the Performing Arts course as a sign of failure and she actively dislikes a large part of the curriculum, which involves dance. Little wonder, then, that she has become disengaged and disruptive. She is on a course which is not consistent with her sense of who she is. This may make her feel that her identity is being undermined. We catch a glimpse of this when she insists on the course leader calling her by her full name.

So how does the research we looked at contribute to our understanding of her situation? Well, we know from the Foster Report (2005) that FE as a progression route takes a far higher percentage of learners from lower socio-economic backgrounds than do school sixth forms. This association of FE with social disadvantage and low educational achievement helps to explain Ellen-Mae's parents' prejudiced view of the sector. They seem to illustrate the idea that FE is a route *for other people's children* (Wolf, 2002, p.56). Ellen-Mae herself is clearly aware of what Swift and Fisher (2012) call *the ambivalent status surrounding vocational education* (p. 207) and therefore finds it difficult to come to terms with it as a suitable option for her. We also know from the research by Thompson (2009) that Ellen-Mae fits the pattern of middle-class learners who enter FE because they've been refused entry to school sixth form because of poor achievement in Year 11. Her case is, therefore, consistent with what the research is telling us. But, unfortunately, that doesn't really help us to work out how best to support her.

And so this was the most difficult question: *what might her teachers be able to do to help her?* Here are a few of the answers you may have come up with.

- **Explore with her the possibility of transferring from the Performing Arts course onto a 're-take' programme so that she can have another go at her Year 11 exams, hopefully improve her results and gain a place on an A level course – perhaps at a sixth form college – where she can get back on track with her original aspirations.**
- **Find out what aspects of the Performing Arts course she dislikes the least (we already know she likes 'reading plays', for example) and develop with her, as far as is possible within curriculum constraints, an individual learning plan.**
- **Attempt to engage her interest through offering her an active role in a group production.**
- **Discuss with her the possibility of transferring to an alternative course at the college.**

All of these involve taking time to listen to the learner. Strategies such as imposing sanctions for non-completion of assignments, lack of punctuality or disruption of others' learning would clearly serve no useful purpose here, since the learner's behaviour is her response to policies and prejudices whose origins lie beyond the individual, the classroom or even the college's control.

Does the current vocational curriculum itself contribute to learner disengagement?

This is a question we raised in Chapter 2, where we considered the possibility that the competence-based curriculum, in place since the introduction of NVQs in 1986, has encouraged learners to see learning as a sort of tick list of 'can do' tasks to be completed, and that this may present as routine and repetitious. Wolf (2011) certainly argues that this is the case. A competence-based tick list approach may well leave learners unaware of the excitement or satisfaction to be gained from deeper levels of learning and understanding. Learning which is purely instrumental – aimed solely at gaining pre-specified skills and knowledge relating to a specific type of employment – is clearly necessary and important. But is it sufficient in itself? Does it meet the full range of learner needs? Is it sufficiently challenging and stimulating? Does it address the development of the wider range of skills that are important for success in adult life? Of the many critics of the instrumental nature of the UK's current vocational curriculum, Richard Pring is one of the most challenging. He advocates a model which he calls 'liberal vocationalism', arguing that job-specific competencies are only part of what is needed to succeed in the world of work. Here is what he has to say:

> *Surely if we focus on what it means to become fully a person ... then there seems no reason why the liberal should not be conceived as something vocationally useful and why the vocationally useful should not be taught in an educational and liberating way.* (Pring, 1999 p. 183)

We encountered the concept of the liberal curriculum in Chapter 7 and saw that it is closely linked to the idea that education should serve not only the needs of employers but also the need for individuals to fulfil their own potential. What Pring means by 'liberal' in the passage just quoted is a more general curriculum such as those followed in Germany and France, which allow learners to engage with a combination of subjects from the arts and sciences alongside their vocationally specific training. In France the *baccalaureate technologique* and the *baccalaureate professionel* prepare students for direct entry into employment while at the same time including these aspects of the liberal curriculum. In Germany the *Abitur*, combines a broad curriculum which prepares students for employment, while retaining the academic rigour considered necessary to qualify them for university entrance. In the UK, however, the academic and vocational routes are largely separate and distinct, and the vocational curriculum contains very little that could be called a broad or liberal education. What Pring is arguing is that this is not the only possible model to adopt, and that a liberal vocational model might better serve the needs of learners and raise their levels of motivation and engagement. This is particularly so in an economic situation where even the successful completion of their competence-based qualification won't necessarily guarantee the learner a job. As Wolf (2011) has argued, learners in FE are fully aware that the accreditation they're working towards doesn't necessarily carry a high value in the employment market. No wonder, then, that some begin to feel it is hardly worth their while trying.

Dylan and the world of work

Let's take our exploration of these issues a little further by examining the case of one particular learner who has little faith in the value of the qualification he is supposed to be working towards and who feels cheated that the college seems unable to support him in acquiring other, broader skills which he believes would give him a competitive edge in the job market.

TASK TASK TASK **TASK** TASK TASK **TASK** TASK TASK **TASK** TASK TASK

As you read Dylan's complaint, consider your answers to the following questions:

- **To what extent does it illustrate the arguments of Wolf and Pring that we've discussed in the section above?**

- **If Dylan had addressed this complaint to you, as his tutor, how would you have answered it? What advice would you give him? Do you agree with any of the points that he makes; and, if so, would you let him know that?**

You asked me why I've been argumentative in class and why I appear uncooperative. So here's my answer. I'm 24 years old and this is my second time round in FE. I came straight from school when I was 16. I got my Level 2 qualification, but that didn't get me into work, so I stayed on and did a Level 3 and that got me into employment when I was 19. Driving a van. I didn't get to use any of the skills I'd learnt at college. And then I was laid off. That was two years ago. I nearly went mental. Bored out of my head. I'd got my Level 3 but I couldn't use any of them skills – couldn't find that sort of work. And I didn't have anything else to offer, did I? So in the end I've had to come back and retrain. And here I go again. I'm getting another set of skills that'll proba-bly go out of date. And what else am I getting? Nothing. Some of the interviews I went for while I was out of work – the ones where the job looked good – they'd ask me stuff – my views on this and that, what I was interested in and that. And I've got nothing to tell them, have I? I haven't had an interesting conversation since I left school. I don't know any more now than I did at 16. So that's my complaint. How can this place say it's preparing us for work when it only helps us with skills that'll go out of date? No help with how to talk to people. No ideas about how to use the time if we're laid off. If I want to learn stuff about how the world works I have to learn it off the telly. So what's going to happen? Maybe I'll get a job when I finish here, but how long will that last for? How to survive stuff like that – that's what you ought to be helping us with. That should be part of it. Shouldn't it?

Discussion

Dylan is expressing some strong feelings here and, to answer our first question, what he says appears to illustrate the arguments of both Wolf and Pring very well. He is fully aware, as Wolf (2011) suggests that many learners are, that the qualifications he's worked towards aren't necessarily valued highly in the employment market. We don't know how this might have affected his behaviour as a learner the first time around, but we get the impression that it's causing problems now. The reservations he expresses about the vocational curriculum echo Pring's argument very closely; particularly Pring's point that *there seems no reason why the liberal should not be conceived as something vocationally useful* (Pring, 1999, p. 183). Although he doesn't use these terms, Dylan is expressing the need for a broader, liberal curriculum which includes 'stuff about how the world works' that will help him succeed in interviews, interact in his workplace, and retain a sense of purpose during periods of unemployment. He is stressing that such an extension to the curriculum would, as Pring argues, be vocationally useful.

So if Dylan had addressed this complaint to you, as his tutor, how would you have answered it? Certainly you would want to begin by thanking him for being so honest. You would probably want to explain to him that the vocational curriculum he's following is set and accredited nationally and that therefore the college has no remit to change it. But you might also offer to use individual tutorial time, if it's available, for introducing some of the subjects he'd like to discuss. You might also advise him of any additional provision he could access in the evenings. Adult Education classes are in short supply these days, but every town has various interest groups, some of which might engage his interest. And if you do agree with any of the points he's made, it will do no harm to tell him so. A feeling that you are both on the same side may be enough to put an end to his negative behaviour. But, if his argumentativeness and lack of cooperation continue, at least having a clearer understanding of his problem will allow you to make sense of this behaviour and not take it personally.

Learners' sense of having no real choice about their progression at 16

In Chapter 2 we touched on how learners' choices may be constrained at 16 and how some may find themselves in FE not out of active choice but almost by default. We've also seen, earlier on in this chapter, how this lack of choice can be linked to issues both of social class and low achievement in school. There is another factor, however, which we need to take into account if we are to fully understand how the notion of 'choice' has become so contested. This factor is the application of *market ideology* to the provision of education and training.

Since the implementation of *The Further and Higher Education Act of 1992*, post-16 provision in the UK has operated within a quasi-market. In other words, school sixth forms must compete with colleges, and colleges must compete with other colleges and with independent training providers. They all must compete for learners (and the funding they attract). But which learners? Schools, which are judged and ranked on the basis of their attainment figures, will naturally wish to retain or attract the ablest learners. They will be less keen to retain the lower achievers. This may well be reflected in the progression advice offered by schools which, suggests research by Fuller and Macfadyen (2012), tends to guide lower achieving learners – and any others they don't wish to retain – towards FE, while advising the most able to stay on at school to take A levels. The research of Swift and Fisher (2012), too, suggests that schools and sixth form colleges recruit or retain learners mostly on the basis of their academic achievement, and that the guidance provided by schools about FE and vocational training is often inadequate or inaccurate. What this means in real terms for some learners is that they may – through poor guidance or through lack of choice – arrive in FE on a vocational course they haven't actively chosen and which doesn't necessarily meet their needs or aspirations. This goes a long way towards explaining some of the behaviours we see from time to time in our classrooms and workshops.

Angel, the reluctant beauty therapist

To understand the ways in which these problems might impact on an individual learner, we're going to look now at the case of Angel, who has suffered from both poor advice and a lack of real choice about her education and training.

TASK TASK TASK **TASK** TASK TASK **TASK** TASK TASK **TASK** TASK TASK

As you read this account by the Counsellor in Student Support Services, consider the following questions:

- **How does the research we've just considered help us to make sense of what has happened to Angel and how she feels about it?**

- **As a teacher, how would you go about supporting and helping Angel?**

Student Support Counsellor's Report

Angel was referred to me by her course tutor who was concerned about Angel's lack of motivation and her generally negative attitude. She suggested to Angel that she come and talk to me, which Angel did. I have since had three further meetings with this student during which she has spoken at length about her current situation and her anxieties. She has given her consent for me to summarise her difficulties in this report in the hope that it may be helpful to teaching staff and others to understand the reasons for her recent behaviour.

It was originally Angel's ambition to be an art therapist. She was good at art at school and gained her highest grade in that subject. Unfortunately her other grades were not sufficiently good to gain her entry to her school's sixth form, where she had hoped to take the A levels she needed to enter the progression route for training as an art therapist. The careers advisor at her school apparently told her that, because of her low grades, her only option was FE. He suggested that if she was interested in becoming a therapist of some sort she should apply for a place on the beauty therapy course. Angel insists that this – unlikely as it sounds – is really what was said (although it seems a bizarre piece of advice, and demonstrates a regrettable lack of understanding on the part of the teacher concerned). At any event, this is Angel's explanation of how she came to be on the beauty therapy course, on the mistaken assumption that the word 'therapy' meant that it would bear at least some relevance to her own aspirations to be an art therapist. This begs the question, of course, of why this misunderstanding on her part was not picked up at the interview and selection stage; and this is something that the section may wish to discuss. Angel lives with her father and her father's girlfriend, neither of whom, according to her, were able to offer her any advice.

Angel tells me that she has no interest in the course she's following and that this is reason for her lack of punctuality and poor attendance. She regrets that she may have been rude and disruptive in class and attributes this behaviour to feelings of frustration and anger that no one will recognise her predicament or try to help her. In my view she is in urgent need of some genuine careers advice, which will make all possible options clear to her. To continue on her current course can only be counter-productive in that it could have the effect of putting her off the idea of any further education and training. I think there are Level 2 and 3 courses in Art and Design offered by the local art school, which is now part of the university. This would seem to be an obvious possibility and I'm surprised that her school was not able to advise her of this.

Discussion

Poor Angel! And our sympathy must go to her teachers, too, who have surely had a rough time of it. This is an extreme example of misinformed or inadequate progression advice from schools about FE provision, a problem identified in the research of Swift and Fisher (2012). But, as the counsellor's report points out, for a learner to find themselves on a course they have no real interest in, it is clear that all is not working well at the recruitment and selection end, either; and so the college, too, must bear some of the blame for Angel's predicament. Her case also illustrates one of the research findings of Fuller and Macfadyen (2012), that progression advice and guidance in schools tends to direct lower achieving learners towards FE. The upshot of all this is that we have a frustrated and angry learner who finds herself somewhere she doesn't want to be and whose behaviour is becoming a barrier not only to her own learning but also to that of others in her class.

So, as a teacher, how would you go about supporting and helping Angel? It looks as though the course tutor has taken the essential first step in directing Angel to someone she can talk to freely about what's troubling her. And the counsellor's suggestion is probably the best one anyone could come up with: that Angel be provided with sound careers and progression advice and supported in making a choice about the next step she takes. The point here is that sometimes, as teachers, we have to pull in specialist advice and help. We can't solve every problem on our own. Where our professional expertise comes in is in recognising what help is needed and making sure our learners are able to access it.

A SUMMARY OF KEY POINTS A SUMMARY OF KEY POINTS A SUMMARY OF KEY POINTS

In this chapter we have:

> looked at what recent research can tell us about possible reasons for learner disengagement and negative behaviour. This research has offered us a number of explanations for the low levels of motivation which FE teachers may encounter in their students.

> identified how all of the explanations offered have something in common in that they locate the origins of (and possible solutions for) the problem at a national policy level. This includes issues around progression, status and choice.

> considered carefully what we, as teachers, can do to support learners affected by these factors, but the chapter underlines the points that learner disengagement should not necessarily nor primarily be assumed to be a result of poor teaching, but may arise as a result of policies and ideologies which lie beyond the teacher's control. That the teacher is still professionally bound to help learners overcome these obstacles is one of the great challenges to the profession.

Branching options

The following three options are designed to provide you with additional opportunities for reflection, analysis and research. You may choose the option which best supports your currently identified needs; or you may find it useful to work through all three tasks.

1. *Reflection*
   - Think about the part of the curriculum that you teach. Would you describe it as competence-based and instrumental?
   - In terms of your own lesson plans, what could be added (or subtracted) to make them more engaging to the learners and more useful in a broader sense, while still preparing them for employment in their chosen vocational area?
   - In what ways could the curriculum across your vocational area be usefully expanded to accommodate a broader more liberal range of learning?

2. *Analysis*
   - Which providers or organisations does your own college compete with? What groups of learners are particularly well served by your college rather than by any of the competitors?
   - How does the college ensure that local schools have adequate and accurate information about the provision it offers?
   - We have discussed how competition might disadvantage some learners by depriving them of real choice. Can you think of any ways in which market competition in post-16 provision might benefit them? Are there any groups in particular who might benefit more than others?

3. *Research*
   - Conduct some research of your own. Ask one of your groups of learners to tell you how and why they came to be in FE and whether it was their first choice for progression.
   - Does what they tell you support any of the research we've looked at in this chapter? If so, in what way?
   - Choose one of the research sources cited in this chapter and find the full text, either through the internet or with the help of your college librarian. What further insights does the full text provide?

REFERENCES AND FURTHER READING REFERENCES AND FURTHER READING

Baird, J., Rose, J. and McWhirter, A. (2012) So tell me what you want: A comparison of FE college and other post-16 students' aspirations. *Research in Post-Compulsory Education,* 15:3 pp. 293–310.

Crawford, M. (2011) *The Case for Working With Your Hands.* London: Penguin.

Foster, A (2005) *Realising the Potential: A Review of the Future Role of Further Education Colleges.* Annesley: DfES.

Fuller, C. and Macfadyen, T (2012) 'What with your grades?' Students' motivation for and experiences of vocational courses in further education. *Journal of Vocational Education and Training*, 64 (1), pp. 87–101.

Pring, R. (1999) *Closing the Gap. Liberal Education and Vocational Preparation*. London: Hodder and Stoughton.

Swift, J. and Fisher, R. (2012) Choosing vocational education: some views from young people in West Yorkshire. *Research in Post-Compulsory Education*, 17 (2), pp. 207–21.

Thompson, R. (2009) Social class and participation in the further education: evidence from the Youth Cohort Study of England and Wales. *British Journal of Sociology of Education*, 30 (1), pp. 29–42.

Wolf, A (2002) *Does Education Matter? Myths about Education and Economic Growth*. London: Penguin.

Wolf, A (2011) *Review of Vocational Education (The Wolf Report)*. London: Department for Education.

Index